Stumbling Souls is an urgent reminder that we are called to care for "the least of these," wherever we find them, whatever shape we find them. From the homeless to the homosexual, from the prisoner to the privileged . . . these lost ones are all around us, waiting to be found. Perhaps it is easier for a war veteran to have the courage to embrace and minister to these stumbling, sordid lives. But as followers of Christ we are all called upon to do just that. Chris Plekenpol's story is one we should emulate. The stories do not all end like a storybook, but it is God's story that he wants to write in all of our lives. If only we will have the courage to follow him in seeking to redeem every stumbling soul.

Curtis V. Hail
President, e3 Partners/I Am Second

Paul loved preaching from the steps of the Temple and in the streets of the marketplace. Paul would have loved Starbucks. Most of us never leave the Temple, much less preach from its steps or dare talk to a stranger about Jesus at Starbucks. It's messy talking to sinners. Paul would have liked Chris, too. Chris gets messy, and in *Stumbling Souls* he shows us how we can't avoid getting our hands dirty as we become more like Christ. Critical book about progressive sanctification!

Drew Dickens
President, Need Him Ministries

Chris Plekenpol is a warrior who takes his faith seriously. He is fearless in the way he tackles the issues that are right in front of us. While others cast a glance towards the poor and feel sorry for a moment, Plekenpol tenaciously attacks this problem with the same love, commitment, and candor that made him a great combat leader. This book is riveting from start to finish and challenged me in the way I view people.

Scott O'Grady
Author, *Return with Honor*

A raw, exciting, and inspiring story of an Army Ranger's journey down the path of the cross. This book will inspire you to believe God for great things in the lives of the broken all around you.

J.D. Greear
Lead Pastor, The Summit Church
Raleigh, North Carolina

STUMBLING SOULS:
IS LOVE ENOUGH?

CHRIS PLEKENPOL

STUMBLING SOULS: IS LOVE ENOUGH?

CHRIS PLEKENPOL

Biblica™

Biblica Publishing
We welcome your questions and comments.

USA   1820 Jet Stream Drive, Colorado Springs, CO 80921 www.authenticbooks.com
India   Logos Bhavan, Medchal Road, Jeedimetla Village, Secunderabad 500 055, A.P.

Stumbling Souls: Is Love Enough?
ISBN-13: 978-1-93406-821-2

Copyright © 2010 by Chris Plekenpol

12 11 10 / 6 5 4 3 2 1

Published in 2010 by Biblica

A catalog record for this book is available through the Library of Congress.

Printed in the United States of America

CONTENTS

ACKNOWLEDGMENTS

Thank you, Jesus, for saving my soul and for being my inspiration to even attempt a book on this. All glory and honor go to you.

Thanks, Merritt Olsen, for all your help in editing and the countless hours at Panera Bread, Café Brazil, and Mama Mia's Pizza. This book wouldn't have happened without you.

Thanks, Mom, for letting me read this to you in the rough draft form over and over again.

Dad, thanks again for helping me with every aspect of this project; from the website to putting this into print, you have been instrumental.

Thanks, Hannah Brann, for the many hours you gave reading this out loud and working through my high-maintenance writing issues.

Thanks to my Advanced Creative Writing Class at Dallas Theological Seminary for putting up with a lot of raw material to make a somewhat polished format. I think we are all indebted to Dr. Reg Grant for his patience and love for us and our Savior!

I love you all.

CHRIS

What good is it, my brothers, if a man claims to have faith but has no deeds? Can such faith save him?

—from the Letter of James

iNTRODucTioN

If you were to visit my seminary campus, you would see several cool statues. There's a rendering of the two Marys at the empty tomb. A giant block of marble exhorts us to simply "Preach the Word." But my favorite statue is a depiction in dull bronze of Jesus washing Peter's feet. This beautiful act has been commemorated over and over—every time another Bible college or seminary orders its own replica. Students, faculty, and other believers take in the sight and are moved by God incarnate serving his creation. But what does it mean for me? As a soldier, I've seen some pretty nasty feet, but I've never washed any of them.

I love seminary. I love sitting under the teaching of amazing, godly people who have been walking with Christ far longer than I have. But I have found, during my time in seminary, that God has revealed as much of himself to me through my interactions with "the least of these" as he has in a classroom.

Some days I would walk out of class and my head would be spinning because of how great and incredible our God is—in theory. But for any disciple, there comes a time when *learning* Christ must become *living* Christ. The greatness of my seminary experience was complete only when the miraculous intangibles of God's character became real in me—when I strove to be Christ to the "sinners" in my world.

But where did I find these "sinners"? Everywhere. Even for the most isolationist among our Christian ranks, the "sinners" are closer than we think. They're our next-door neighbors, the person one cubicle over at the office, and the barista at the local coffee shop. Then there are those really big-time dirty sinners: the drug users, hard partiers, sexual deviants, and the like (some of whom may also be your next-door neighbors, coworkers, and coffee-shop employees). They've racked up so much sin and destroyed their lives to the point that even their mothers have turned them away. It's possible that many of these people have lined the pews of your own church. You may even have shaken hands with them, though chances are you didn't know the extent of their depravity.

Let's be honest here. Some people are dirtier than others. They lead more destructive lives. They hurt more people. But truth is it takes the same amount of blood to wash them clean as it does to wash me.

When Christ went to the cross to pay the penalty for our sin, the wrath of God was satisfied for *all* sin. If only "sinners" would understand what that means to them, not only would they be saved from hell, but they could wrap themselves up in this amazing love and experience a full life in the here and now. If only the saved would understand what this truth means, then they themselves would be the bearers of this amazing love to the dirtiest of sinners—even to themselves.

This book follows my heartfelt, sometimes messy, attempts to translate orthodoxy (right thinking) into orthopraxy (right action). Through my interaction with both "sinners" and "saints," I'll examine what it means to live out some of the verses we usually skim—you know, the passages that require action from our faith. These are the kinds of verses that are rarely used on coffee cups, refrigerator magnets, or bumper stickers.

You see, the facet of that seminary statue that people don't seem to notice is how filthy Peter's feet really are. Can we serve as Christ served without getting our hands dirty? Without smelling the stench of sin?

Wealth brings many friends,
but a poor man's friend deserts him.

—from the Book of Proverbs

CHAPTER 1: HOMELESS

Homeless people tend to be homeless for a reason. Society ostracizes them because they don't play a productive part in the real world, yet many of these "parasites" expect us "hosts" to give them a handout. I stood and watched the homeless man who, only moments before, had attended my church's monthly newcomers' meeting. His goal clearly wasn't church membership but rather to unburden the church from its overabundance of turkey, bread, chips, and pickles. He understood social dynamics well enough to know that a church staff member wouldn't kick out the smelly guy in the sweatpants from the newcomers' meeting or deprive him of the remaining boxed lunches. He had struck gold and was carrying his bounty back to his world.

I thought, *What a nice gesture*, but I couldn't take my eyes off the figure walking away, and something inside me stirred. I tried to quell the desire to stop him and find out about his life. Honestly, I didn't really want to know. I mean, let's face it; involving myself in this man's problems could be the beginning of a parasitic relationship that would drain my wallet and my emotions. Was I really ready to open myself up to that kind of a nuisance? I never failed to give a homeless man a dollar when asked. Well, maybe not every time. Okay, maybe when I accidentally looked a homeless man in the eye and something pierced my soul—that's when I'd give him a dollar to make that awkward feeling go away. I'd feel better and walk away, congratulating myself for the good deed I'd done. I could even share the tale of my generosity with others if I wanted to feel really swell. As I stood on the steps weighing the decision, I felt justified for a moment watching the man's hefty frame slump away, his head cast down toward the ground. Clearly, a lack of food wasn't this guy's problem.

My megachurch had helped a poor soul, if only for a day. We made the world a better place. This fact should have vindicated me. That's what the church is about, you know, helping those who can't help themselves. Granted, it really works out conveniently when they show up, take a meal, and then leave. We get the gratification of doing something good, and we don't have to get really entangled in the mess. But even by simply contributing to this man's free meal, I had been a part of God's work. I was a soldier in the army of the Lord! With that feeling tucked into my soul, I should've climbed into my car with my friends and driven into Uptown Dallas without a care in the world, watching Mercedes, BMWs, and sometimes even

Ferraris drive by and not given the man a second thought. That's what normally would've happened.

But that day something awakened deep inside of me—maybe in the place where a small filling of the Holy Spirit resides. The part of me that is not yet dead, that still has a heartbeat for God every now and then. You may have this too—that part that comes alive in worship and causes you to weep or laugh with joy or gives you the tingles and shivers when someone else does what God has called hm or her to do.

Sometimes I realize that I'm like Dr. Seuss's Grinch, that this part of my heart is three sizes too small. I took a good look at the figure receding in the distance—male, black, probably about forty-five years old. How long had it been since he had a friend? Did anyone even care enough to ask his name? All of a sudden, I was overcome by the wonder and beauty of the cross—the reality that, though I deserve death, God has ransomed me from his wrath by his Son. And just like the Grinch, I felt this once-dead part of me starting to grow. There was no restraining it.

I looked over at my friend Bill. "Is that guy homeless?"

Bill shifted his weight and peered over my shoulder. "Yeah, he's just asking for food. Surprised we don't see him panhandling here."

"That's not the right attitude. Somebody should reach out to that guy."

"Better you than me."

Before I knew it, my legs started walking after this stranger who had no idea of the welling up of *something* in my soul.

"Hey," I called after him. He didn't turn around. He kept walking, likely thinking that no one would ever call after him, and if someone did they might be trying to take the food back or harass him in some way.

"Hey!" I called again. "Hey, buddy!"

He turned slowly. He looked me up and down, noting my pressed, pinstriped pants and button-down shirt with suspicion. Obviously, we'd never met. He stealthily slid the bag of food into his worn sweatpants. "Yes?" he finally replied.

"Do you have lunch plans?" I asked as if I might be bothering him or interrupting his incredibly busy schedule of sitting somewhere on a street corner.

"No," came the terse reply.

"Do you want to go to lunch with me and some of my friends?"

He smiled, revealing a gap between his front two teeth large enough to accommodate a compact car. "Yeah. Yeah, I'd like that."

"I'm Chris, by the way." I slapped him on the shoulder and turned to find my friends. A handshake may have been a better gesture, but I wasn't quite there yet.

"I'm James."

The fatherless child is snatched from the breast;
the infant of the poor is seized for a debt.

—from the Book of Job

CHAPTER 2: PEI WEI

Pei Wei is a great, inexpensive place to eat. I smiled wide, walking into the restaurant, knowing that James would have food to spare and people who cared for him for an afternoon. I mean, here's a man who doesn't know how God will provide his next meal, and I get to be the guy God uses to do that. I looked across the table and watched James survey the rest of the group from church. I got the impression that he was expecting us to talk around the elephant in the room. Maybe he would've been more comfortable if we'd confined the conversation to surface-level pleasantries, but I've never been one to avoid the awkward, so I decided to just go for it.

"So, James, where're you from?" I asked.

"I'm from New Orleans. I came to Dallas right after Katrina."

"Wow. Really?" I asked.

"Go on," Bill said. He eyed James with suspicion. Bill was always like that. I'd grown to accept his pessimistic outlook toward humanity. He'd seen a lot in his time on the Narcotics Task Force and had lived a hard life. He'd arrested drug addicts, sex offenders, and murderers of the worst kind, and his radar for con artists was always on high alert.

Every now and then Bill would share stories with me of what he'd experienced in his thirteen years on the force. That would be enough to drive even the most stable men to drink. His time in AA had been an incredible blessing and something for which he always thanked God. But eleven years sober, he still bore the scars of working the streets. I could tell he wasn't exactly sure what to make of James, and I couldn't wait to ask him later about his thoughts on this man who sat across from me.

James looked down at his food while he talked, as if to make sure it didn't try to escape his plate. "The Superdome was rough—so crowded. People had guns and were robbin' one another all over the place. I watched a couple women get raped. Seriously, I was afraid for my life there. It was especially bad when they turned off the water."

"Why'd they do that?" I asked.

"Well, you know the water had become contaminated and stuff. So they shut it down, but when you shut down the water, you shut down the plumbing. So the Superdome became a cesspool. Imagine it. No drinking water. All the toilets filled with human waste, no plumbing, thirty thousand people crammed into one area with no police or anything. It was crazy. I'm just glad I'm outta there."

I sat there dumbfounded that something like this could happen in America. Could people really be that sick and twisted? In seminary, we've learned about the depravity of humanity and what happens to people without the common grace of God: stuff like government, family, and institutions. Without it, even America can look like *The Lord of the Flies.*

"Wow," Christina and Michael Riley said in unison. Christina had been uncharacteristically silent up to this point. Michael Riley's quiet demeanor on the other hand was true to form. We all looked at each other and back at James.

"What did you do before Katrina? Where did you grow up?" Christina asked, changing the subject.

"Hmmm, well, I grew up in Virginia Beach. I was kind of a beach bum. I'd go out my backdoor and step right on the beach. My dad died of double pneumonia when I was nine. I loved that man more than life itself."

James fidgeted with his chopsticks and subsequently picked up a fork. He looked up for a moment before casting his eyes back down at his plate. Then he revealed something that I didn't expect.

"I'm a homosexual."

All eyes shifted to James, but there was no alarm. The group just gave him its full attention.

James continued: "A while back, I decided to leave the lifestyle, but that decision hasn't quite affected my desires yet. As much as I read the Bible trying to find a loophole for my sexual preferences, I never find one. I've been in a bad place for a long time, but I really want to please God."

James paused. His pained expression made me wonder if there was something more to the story. He looked at his entrée that lay before him. Rice dispersed by half-eaten chicken. I guess I figured that a man who didn't know when he would see his next meal would consume free food a bit more—enthusiastically. His chopsticks lay over the bowl. He'd given up trying to use them and now fiddled with a fork. He looked up and into the eyes of those whom he had just met, strangers who had given of their time and resources to grant him the gift of lunch.

"I'm HIV positive."

He let that settle on the group as if the shock of the statement might cause tremors in the restaurant or send us scattering like cockroaches in the light.

"So, there are a lot of gays and lesbians who go to the church that are in the same condition. You're not special," Bill said in his usual gruff-but-loving manner.

James smiled, and I was relieved that Bill hadn't scared him off—yet. I decided to keep the conversation moving.

"So when did you become gay?" I didn't know how else to ask that question, but James didn't miss a beat.

"When my dad died—that's where my life started to turn. My mom, who really didn't know what to do with me, sent me away to boys' camp. Well, I got up one night at like three in the morning to go to the bathroom, and I heard some things happening in another tent, and I went to check it out. I opened the tent flap, and there were some men who were," he paused, "doing some things to each other. They saw me and motioned for me to join them."

"Did you?" I asked, a little too involved in the story.

"I did."

I grimaced. It had probably happened about thirty years ago, but I still wanted things to play out differently for young James.

"Right, well, what did you do after that?" I asked.

"I went to culinary school and was a cook in the army for a while. I went to Bible college and was a worship leader for a while.

The guilt of my sin was pretty heavy. I turned to drugs to numb the guilt, the whole time still searching for that loophole that made being gay okay."

"How did you wind up in New Orleans?" I asked as Bill stared at him enough to make me uncomfortable.

"Oh, you know, just trying to find work somewhere. I ended up in New Orleans and now here. But the toughest thing about being here is not having an ID card. I couldn't keep my job at the Melrose Hotel . . ." James's voice trailed off as he stared at his fingernails.

"Why don't you just go to the DMV and get one?" I asked.

"Don't have any ID to get an ID. I'm hoping to get my birth certificate soon. I hear that there is a Stewpot downtown that I can get a temporary ID at, but that won't get me a job. Some corporations are pretty serious about this ID thing."

"What kind of job you looking for?" I felt like the twenty questions guy and could sense Bill getting annoyed.

"Anything to do with cooking. It's difficult to find cooking jobs when you have HIV, but I don't mind bartending either. You can make good money doing that. I've done it a couple times and did great on tips."

"Chris, enough questions," Bill said, cutting his eyes toward me. "He hasn't even really started eating, and you and I are almost done. Hey, James, we have a men's Bible study that meets every Monday night if you want to come. ****, you tell me where to pick you up, and I'll drive you there myself."

It was all I could do to keep my mouth shut. Bill had actually invited James to the Bible study. A part of me was excited. I couldn't believe Bill, of all people, invited James. Wonders never cease.

James was pleasantly surprised. "I'd love to. I gotta tell you, I really expected to be judged for everything I told you. Y'all are different," he said, shaking his head.

I laughed. "That is the last thing you'll get from us, James." Now, I said that out loud, but on the inside I wasn't so sure. I mean, would I bring this guy home to meet my mom? Not in a million years. Or maybe that says something about my mom and not me. I don't know; I didn't feel weird sitting across from James, but the huge weight starting to rest on my shoulders told me if we continued to be nice to James that, like a stray dog, he would be coming back around for another handout.

"****, you don't have to worry about our judgment," Bill said emphatically. "I've woke up too many mornings not knowin' who I was layin' next to and not knowin' how I got there and scannin' the room for condom wrappers to piece together the night before." Bill's candor wasn't for the faint of heart. Women who didn't know Bill's softer side were always put off by his lack of tact. Christina had known Bill for years and didn't flinch. His demeanor made me feel like I was back in Iraq strapping on my gear ready to go out in sector to find bad guys. So, for me, his language came off as normal, but the expression on James's face told me that Bill made him more than uncomfortable.

We wrapped up lunch and headed outside to the car. James went out first, and as the door shut behind him, I paused and softly elbowed Bill in the ribs. "What in the world? I thought you were against helping the homeless? Did you have a change of heart?"

"No, you'll see. This guy ain't for real. You need to learn somehow. You may have been in Iraq and fought terrorists, but you don't know Americans like I know 'em. He probably won't even show up."

Now there's the Bill I knew.

"I'll call you after we drop James off."

James and I got into Christina's SUV, and we drove through Dallas to a small church where he stashed some of his stuff. As we drove, he talked about the difficulty of living on the streets. We dropped him off, and Christina handed him a twenty. I was glad that she was helping him out; I didn't feel like being the only one to sacrifice.

I called Bill.

"Hey, man, what do you think?" I asked.

"It's possible that this guy could be legit, but I doubt it. I've seen it too many times. Remember I used to feed the homeless with a local church for about two years steady. Then, in my third year, I realized that I was feeding the same people over and over. I was enabling them. As long as they were getting three hots and a cot they wouldn't do anything different. I figured the more miserable it was, the quicker they'd take the initiative to get off the streets."

"Bill, this guy's a Katrina victim. It's different," I said.

"Chris, after Katrina, Dallas was dumped on by a bunch of Katrina sponges. Many were already in the system on welfare. They're not gonna change just because there was a little water where they used to squat. So they move to Dallas and set up shop here. James might not even be from New Orleans. He just got the stories from others that were transplanted here. It's profitable to be a Katrina sponge. Everybody's diggin' deep into their pockets to help these people out. Many need the help, but a large percentage don't."

"Man, I tried to decipher truth from fiction. I mean that is a lot of story to make up for him not to be legit."

"He has a lot of time and a lot of people to con for a handout," Bill said.

"James talked about how good God was and how this lunch was an answer to prayer."

"I know, good technique, ain't it? My money is on that this was another ploy to get us to sympathize. I thought there might be some manipulation involved, but I know you want to believe the best in people. I, on the other hand, always extend the olive branch with a reserve tactical plan to kill if needed."

"I guess we'll figure it out if he shows on Monday."

We exchanged pleasantries and hung up.

Christina told me not to worry about Bill and that we did the right thing. I agreed and let Bill's suspicion roll off my back.

After Christina dropped me off back at church, I got into my car and sat in the parking lot. *This is the Christian life.* We told James we wanted to love and serve him; well, at least I did; Christina gave him twenty bucks, and Bill offered to drive him to Bible study.

As I pulled away in my Saturn, the thoughts continued to ping-pong in my head. *What if Bill was right?* James could be pulling the wool over my eyes. But could I judge a man's heart? I had to have only one concern: to be the hands and feet of Jesus. We do the will of Christ when we invite those who can't pay us back. If we invite our friends, brothers, relatives, or rich neighbors, they may also invite us in return, and this itself will be our reward. The Lord will reward us for extending hospitality to those who can't repay.[1]

I had a real sense that I'd done the right thing. I wanted to pat myself on the back for the effort. We didn't judge him. We gave him something to eat. We listened without threatening to put a call in to the morality police. I guess that was my way of saying, "I love you," to an HIV-positive, homeless homosexual.

However, I sensed that God was calling me to something more.

The poor are shunned even by their neighbors,
but the rich have many friends.

—from the Book of Proverbs

CHAPTER 3: SPF7

Monday came fast. Greek homework had vise-gripped my frontal lobe, and I forced myself to focus on the task of writing out Greek verb paradigms. At 6:45 PM, I hurried to the seminary to ready the President's Room in time for the twelve men who would soon show for our weekly Bible study. The President's Room was normally reserved for the board of directors of the seminary to plot out the course and direction for the school. Located in Café Koine, the seminary's coffee shop, it was the perfect place to host men coming straight from work who might need a boost of caffeine to endure a two-and-a-half-hour Bible study.

The walls were decorated with seminary greats, past and present. Andy Stanley and Chuck Swindoll stared at me from their places on the wall. I wondered for a moment if I could ever make an impact like those guys have. The door opened, interrupting my thoughts. Bill walked in, followed by James.

"Hey, guy." Bill always called me "guy." At first that annoyed me, but with most things, you get used to the way people are. I always thought you called someone "guy" when you forgot his name and were looking for a subtle substitute. Bill called everyone "guy." That was his way. Bill's opinionated personality encased a heart that really wanted to see people experience the life change that had taken him from an alcoholic to a man of character—rough character. The Holy Spirit still had some Mexican whorehouses, gunfights, and hard drinking to sandblast from his past in order to smooth out the rough edges. I think that's why I like Bill so much. He's a straight shooter with no pretense. He grew up in Highland Park, Dallas's elite area; however, no one would ever confuse him for a pretentious corporate executive with the Harley T-shirt, bald head, and goatee that he sported today.

"Hey, Bill." I backslap-hugged him.

James followed closely. He didn't look homeless tonight. His polo shirt was clean, and although he wore sweatpants, he looked like he could have been a businessman who had just come from his home gym. His cleaner attire was contrasted by his demeanor. He looked droopy. I'm not sure how else to put it. He resembled Eeyore, from Winnie-the-Pooh, after losing his tail.

"Hey, James," I said and smiled as wide as possible, hoping to elicit a similar response. James mumbled something incoherent. I moved forward and wrapped my arms around him and gave him a big hug. He stood there as if doing me a favor by offering me his frame to squeeze. The other men filtered into the room. Some gave James a firm handshake, others simply a nod. Only a few actually knew James was homeless. We sat down as I got the equipment ready for our study of Matthew 8.

"Hey, everyone. Quick introduction. This is my buddy James— James, everyone." The group responded with a hearty hello. James canted his head a little and nodded. I continued: "James, this group is called SPF7. That stands for Safe Place to Fall at 7 PM. What we do here is inductive, methodical Bible study, and there is no condemnation for anything you want to share. We really mean that. We're rockin' through the book of Matthew. We started in November in Matthew chapter 6, and now here in late April we are in Matthew 8. I know we're not exactly setting any land-speed records for moving through the Bible, but we're growing in our relationships and in our own faith walks. As we read the text, we will put observations up here on the Excel spreadsheet," I motioned to the spreadsheet projected on the wall, "while the Scripture will be up on the other projector."

James nodded as if digital Bible study had been around forever and that my explaining it was tiresome. We prayed and started going over the specifics of the man with leprosy who asked Jesus to heal him after he gave the Sermon on the Mount. At first James remained quiet, but as the men started opening up, James made a couple of contributions, and his face became—less droopy. *Maybe he just needed to feel comfortable to open up*, I thought.

"Guys," James interjected, "I'm HIV positive so I know how this man with leprosy feels." Out came the feelers. I could see James's eyes trying to read the faces of those around him. He leaned back in his chair and let his bomb drop. Would they accept or reject? I wondered how many times he had been told to leave Starbucks or some other air-conditioned facility in Dallas when his small coffee or beverage ran out. Our world could be so cruel. None of the men flinched, and I felt a little pride creep into my smile.

"That sucks," Trey, a twenty-six-year-old professional computer hacker (the legal kind), chimed in. I initially met Trey several months ago at a small-group meeting from church. Forty of us had been crammed into a one-room loft for a Bible study. Okay, I know what you're thinking. Forty isn't that small. But somehow it worked, and it was a great place to meet people from church. Trey stuck out among the crowd, primarily because he looked like a *GQ* model. He had an incredible physique and blue eyes that cut through women like a laser through toilet paper. Women all across the DFW Metroplex had fallen all over themselves vying for his attention. However, the man wasn't merely eye candy; he was smart. Wicked smart. He reminded me of Will, the guy Matt Damon played in the movie *Good Will Hunting*. Trey didn't have a college degree, but he had already done very, very well for himself in the computer security industry by merely reading all the manuals. He was a level of genius few could fathom. On top of that, the guy really loved God. He had incredible insight as well as vulnerability about his own weaknesses, which usually manifested themselves in women being unable to resist his unique allure. Over the past couple of months, I had gotten to know Trey and found his personality very refreshing. If Trey's acceptance was any indication of what the guys could handle, James would be right at home.

"This man had desperation," James said. "He willed himself to find Jesus even if it meant coming into a society that feared catching his disease. He was willin' to try anything. I'm the same way. I gave up the homosexual lifestyle a while back, but that doesn't mean I don't need healing."

"Well said, James," I said, trying to hide my astonishment of his articulating a Bible passage so well. He'd clearly paid attention at Bible college.

To be honest, when Bill volunteered to bring James to SPF7, I hesitated. Would James's presence become a burden to the other members? I dismissed the thought, choosing instead to see what would happen when we mixed two different worlds. Could it change us? Would we become callous or more like Christ? Could I really put my faith in action and lead other men to do so? I was so focused on how SPF7 would benefit James. I never thought that James's insight would be exactly what we needed.

We finished the Bible study late, as usual, and I asked for prayer requests. After about forty-five minutes of sharing the entire gamut of issues men face, James spoke.

"I'm tired of being on the streets. I'm tired of not knowing where to eat, tired of not working," he stated softly, staring at the table. "I know that God has a plan, and somehow he's working me through that right now. But I need money for laundry and money for a place to stay." He was desperate to avoid eye contact at all costs.

This was tough. James had a clear need and was putting it out there. It felt strange to hear someone in the group just simply express his financial needs to men who could do something about it. I glanced around the room and realized that many of the regulars were probably struggling with the same feeling. Most of us had never interacted with a homeless person before. We'd seen people like James on the streets and ignored them or gave the obligatory dollar to ease our consciences; yet here was a forty-five-year-old homeless man surrounded by twenty-six- to forty-five-year-old, pretty well-to-do men. Something in my soul loosened my wallet. I didn't want to make a big deal about it, but I could not sit there and do nothing, knowing this man would sleep on the street that night while I slept in my comfy loft bed. The tension in the room mounted as we all wondered what we should do with this elephant.

My men's group had rallied around causes before. We once purchased a laptop for a down-and-out seminary student. That was a great achievement for our little group. But this was different. This was a problem that wouldn't be solved by a one-time cash donation. Something inside me quivered as I wondered how we could continue as a Bible study if we didn't meet the material needs of our group. Really, what would be the point? If we talked about how we were going to be there for each other and support one another, didn't that mean we must give our lives to one another? For that night, we could get away with just giving some cash to fight off the guilt, to grant us a temporary feeling of being holier than we really were. But what about after that? What would be required of us?

"Wow, James, we will definitely add that to the prayer list. Honestly, I don't even know how to respond to that."

Scott-Michael, whom I had met in Iraq several years ago and who now lived in Irving, spoke up. "I can get you a cell phone, James; that'll probably help with getting a job. We can even get you a prepaid one."

"Thanks, Scott-Michael," James said.

"Men, let's go to the Lord in prayer over all the stuff we have brought up tonight." I said, "Bill, would you mind leading us?"

We prayed, and afterward a couple of the men gathered around me and stuffed my palm with cash. I would be taking James back to the streets.

"James, you want to go to Café Brazil?"

"Yeah," James said. His face had lost the droop for a moment and now held a smile.

We left the seminary and drove to Café Brazil located across the street from Southern Methodist University, one of the richest schools in the country. I wondered what they would think of him, and for a moment I had to shake off the insecurity of what someone might think of me for hanging out with James. *Man, I have a long way to go to reach Christlikeness.* I don't even feel comfortable taking a homeless man to a coffee shop, where the style is to look homeless anyway. James ordered an omelet, and I had a fruit plate. We exchanged small talk; I handed him the money from SPF7 and then decided it was time to take him back to his street corner. We left Café Brazil and the elite of SMU en route to a part of the city where rape and murder were commonplace. At that moment, my comfy garage apartment in one of the nicest neighborhoods in Dallas became the albatross hanging around my neck.

I thought briefly about a really cool chapel message I had heard in my first semester at seminary. The pastor was a DTS grad who was also Pentecostal. He pastored a culturally relevant church in Deep Ellum. Deep Ellum is about as eclectic as it gets and is known for being an artists' hangout. Bars, dance clubs, and tattoo parlors lined the streets. This guy had a heart to reach people who were really broken.

It was incredible. He talked about seeing a certain homeless guy on the street day after day. He and his wife had taken him to lunch and befriended him, and then one day, they asked him to move in. I remember picking my jaw off the floor as he spoke about ministering to a dying homeless man in the last few months of his life. His body finally gave way to the harsh wear and tear of living on the streets, and that couple was there to comfort him at his life's end. After that chapel service I remained in my seat. I didn't move. But something in me looked at that guy with a sort of awe. Here is a guy who gets it. He has a track record with Christ of taking care of those who can't take care of themselves. I have a feeling that Jesus would have looked at this guy and said, "You are very near to the kingdom of God."

I slowed the car to a halt at the corner of Cadiz and Ervay. I added fifty bucks from my wallet to James's meager housing fund and felt a little better—for the moment.

He who oppresses the poor shows contempt for their Maker, but whoever is kind to the needy honors God.

—from the Book of Proverbs

CHAPTER 4: BRIT

"Hey, Brit, how are you?" I pulled Brit in close for a man hug in the hallway of the Todd Academic Building.

"Bro, I'm getting smoked in Hebrew. It's getting rough." When I was hanging with Brit, I always felt a little closer to the beach. It was like he was on his way to wax down his surfboard in his garage—that's because he's a surfer and he uses his garage as a surfboard workshop. The transition to the fast-paced Dallas world had not settled well on his surfer soul. Something was lost in translation from the crashing waves along the north shore of Maui to the traffic and masses of humanity in the metroplex. Although his body was in Dallas, his heart was still anchored in Honolua Bay.

"I hear that. I'm barely making it with my Greek exegetical. Seminary is not for the faint of heart," I said.

"How's that Bible study of yours going?" he asked.

"It's awesome. You're not going believe it. I actually have a homeless guy coming."

Brit grinned. He was accustomed to the unreal happening in my world. "Nice. How did that happen?"

"Met him at church, asked him to lunch; then Bill asked him to come to the Bible study, and he's been coming for a month or so. Pretty incredible, actually. I would love it if you could come."

"Bro, I don't know if I have time."

"Brit, please come to my Bible study." I smiled, trying to be as manipulative and persuasive as possible. "I need you there, man."

"I've got to spend more time with my wife," Brit countered.

"Look, you keep talking about doing real ministry. Well, here's your chance. Come and make a difference. I need you there. I don't know how to handle this homeless guy by myself," I said.

I watched Brit's interest pique. He loved the fact that I taught the Bible to a rough crowd. Having a homeless guy show up made it even more appealing.

"Yeah," he said.

For a moment Brit looked like he was doing chaos-theory equations in his head. "I'll be there. What time?"

"Seven o'clock," I said and smiled victoriously. I respected Brit a lot. Having him at Bible study was like adding Yoda to your Jedi collection.

"Tonight right, bro?" Brit asked.

"Yep."

"Okay, see you there."

I arrived at the President's Room as normal. Bill brought James again. Brit eased his way into the room and unassumingly sat down at the table next to Michael Riley. He eyeballed the gathering of men from different backgrounds. I could tell he was intrigued.

"Men, let's go ahead and open our Bibles up to the book of Matthew." We analyzed Matthew chapter 9. Brit put aside his tranquil, laid-back surfer demeanor for a moment and became impassioned.

"Check it out. This is what I'm talking about is wrong with the church today. Look at what Jesus says in Matthew 9:12: 'It is not those who are healthy who need a physician, but those who are sick.'[1] The contemporary church is so full of those who think they are healthy, and they keep away the people who know they are sick. It's crap, man. It's crap."

"To be honest, I'm sick. I need help, but y'all are the first ones who have reached out to me," James added.

"Well, James, I'm glad that we can right a major wrong in a small way with how we are treating you," I said.

James nodded.

When the discussion was over, we took prayer requests. I watched Brit as James shared his needs. I thought I saw Brit's eyes turn glassy for a moment when James explained his hope to sleep under some sort of shelter the next time it rained.

We wrapped up, and I left the rest of the guys in the seminary parking lot and made my way to Café Brazil for some late-night studying. I got a phone call from one of the SPF7 guys as I pulled into my parking space.

"Hey, man, what do you think about my putting James up in the Fairmont Hotel? I prepaid the room in cash so that he couldn't run up my credit card. I figured a night off the street and a chance to shower and sleep in a comfy bed might do him some good. Besides I got a good deal—seventy-five bucks for the night."

"That's incredible. Thanks for doing that. I know that James will really appreciate it."

"I know that in my head, but he didn't seem too grateful."

"Yeah, that's just the way he is. He's just kinda—droopy. I think I might be too if I were homeless."

"Good point. I was just letting you know and wanted to see what you thought. I'm heading home. See you later."

You only live once I guess. Putting a homeless guy in a fancy hotel for a night doesn't solve his situation, but it does let you rest easy for a night knowing that you are trying to do something. James's presence forced us to face the issue of what to do with a man with no home, job, or way to provide. It made us uneasy, and I think we needed that. Complacency robs us of the opportunity to face our feelings of guilt for having something when others don't. We could keep throwing money at the feeling for a while, but eventually something would have to give. I wondered how my own heart would handle interaction with the other side of the tracks on a regular basis. My cell phone vibrated, interrupting my thoughts.

"Bro," Brit's voice surfed through the phone. "Thanks for making me come tonight. I'm blown away by James. He and I are going to have lunch this week."

"Great! Let me know how it goes."

"Yeah, pretty awesome. I'll give you some feedback, bro. Back to Hebrew."

This could really work. We can make a difference. It just starts with one person, right? I sat in the parking lot for a moment longer and recalled my first encounter with homeless people in Atlanta, Georgia. I was about sixteen or seventeen years old on a Lutheran youth group retreat. Young Lutherans from around the country converged on Atlanta, and at night after the conference we hung out by this big fountain near the Georgia Dome. Homeless people came and talked to us. I'm sure I emptied my pockets of whatever I had. I couldn't understand why they didn't have a job. My whole perception of America broadened in that moment. I always figured this was the land of opportunity. If you were willing to work, you could reach your dreams. Evidently that wasn't so. After that experience I always made a point to give money to homeless guys. It was like my way of putting an end to poverty. Strangely, although I actually started receiving a paycheck and multiple raises, I still could manage only a dollar for them most of the time.

When I lived in Colorado Springs while still in the army, my buddies and I bought ten pizzas every Saturday and handed them out to the homeless at a recreation park. I wanted to get to know them. But even that was difficult, because all I could do was listen and eventually leave. I would buy a bus pass every now and then, take them to Subway a time or two, but again, my generosity ended there. It was controlled. I would meet the homeless on neutral turf, and we would just talk.

This was different. I had invited a homeless man into my inner circle.

Whoever heard me spoke well of me, and those who saw me commended me,

because I rescued the poor who cried for help,
and the fatherless who had none to assist him.

—from the Book of Job

CHAPTER 5: TREY

I parked my car as close as possible to the door of Café Koine. Monday had come quicker than I had expected. I stepped outside and immediately felt perspiration gather on my forehead. I could go from zero to drenched-in-my-own-sweat in less than ten minutes in the one-hundred-plus-degree heat and humidity that Dallas provided its citizens.

Opening my trunk, I pulled out the second laptop computer and the two projectors that I owned for the purpose of conducting the most interactive Bible study possible. Thankfully, the computer equipment didn't seem like it suffered damage due to its exposure to the heat. I didn't fair so well. In less than thirty seconds my shirt was wet enough to stick to my chest. I looked like I had stumbled upon sprinklers. I quickly walked to the safety of the air-conditioned building. After grabbing a café white mocha, a necessary remedy to the overcompensation of the seminary's arctic chill, I walked over to the President's Room and began to set up the projectors and ready the room for SPF7.

Brit arrived with James in tow wearing a T-shirt and ripped sweatpants. Brit had bought him a cup of coffee and two slices of pepperoni pizza for dinner from Café Koine. I smiled as they walked in and gave Brit an enthusiastic hug and backslap, while James greeted me with an obligatory handshake. He went limp like a dead fish as I pulled him close for a handshake-backslap. I was mildly irritated that he didn't smile and return my gesture as heartily. Then I remembered that he had most likely spent the entire day playing hide-and-seek with coffee-shop managers and store owners trying to find somewhere cool to escape the scorching Dallas day without being whisked away. Perhaps intimacy could not be microwaved.

The Bible study started with the usual gusto. We continued to walk through the book of Matthew as men related the text to their lives. Almost everyone had some sort of heartache to share with the group. Even with a guy like James present, they opened up and talked freely. I don't think the magnitude of his presence had really set in yet. When it came time for prayer requests, we went around the room. James went last.

"Whatcha got, James?" I asked.

"Last week I told Chris that I got a job at Landry's—you know, the upscale seafood restaurant. A server can make up to a thousand dollars a week there if he plays his cards right."

"That's great," Brit said and smiled at James.

"But after only a week of working there, I got laid off," James retorted.

The initial excitement we felt upon hearing he had gotten a job was replaced with a swift punch in the gut. James told us directly, "I need an ID. I can't get another job without an ID. I need God to do something."

Trey asked with vigor in his voice, "James, are you telling me that all you need is an ID?"

James nodded.

Trey's next statement thundered with resolution. "This is not a problem. Between Bill and me, we know too many people for something as simple as an ID to hold you back from getting a job."

The room was silent for a moment. I got chills.

We called him "The Trey Show." We'd heard stories of Trey's work colleagues naming him that, and we all felt it was appropriate. He truly was a one-man show. At twenty-six, his youth made most executives underestimate him, and Trey ate them for lunch. His intelligence gave him little patience for those in the computer industry who did not have his technical expertise and foresight. He was known for not being afraid to tell off a top executive and then walk out, only to have that executive call him back, apologize, and do whatever it was that "The Trey Show" recommended. So, not only could Trey hack with the best minds in America and look *GQ*, but he had fearless ambition as well as a love for God and people, which clearly showed in his desire to make a difference.

The men around the table, who moments before feebly stared at their hands, now all gave their attention to "The Trey Show," whose face looked as if it were ready to be carved into granite. I felt awed by his conviction to do something. Why hadn't I been that resolute? I was thankful that someone was, and inwardly I was starting to gain momentum in the direction God was pushing me. There was hope. People really can care more about others than themselves. Trey had his own concerns. He found a new job and soon would move to San Francisco. He was trying to get everything together for his new life. Yet, he was going to take pause and figure this thing out.

Trey didn't know it, but he challenged me. I knew soon that I would have to take a risk. I would have to take a stand for something—something more than leading a good Bible study. This wasn't simply about the formality of an ID card. It was about doing for a man what he could not do for himself—about standing in the gap for a man who could not stand for himself. Doing what the church was called to do: be the hands and feet of Christ to the marginalized in our society. I think Trey did for me exactly what the Bible talks about when it exhorts us to think of ways we can motivate one another toward love and doing the right thing.[1]

Honestly, I didn't know how that would play out, but as the tears edged my eyes with the surreal reality of men being willing to inconvenience themselves to take care of one another, I realized that God meant for us to live inconvenient lives. I'm starting to believe that is when life is most lived. Trey wasn't afraid of the challenge. He wasn't afraid to try. He wasn't afraid to commit. He put his cards on the table.

I prayed I could do the same. When neither sun nor stars appeared for many days and the storm continued raging, we finally gave up all hope of being saved.

—from the Book of Acts

CHAPTER 6: RAIN

It doesn't really rain in Dallas in the summer. Most summers we dream of green grass like we dream of snow in the winter. Yet for weeks on end it rained. You know the kind of rain I'm talking about. The cumulus clouds send rain, drenching the neighborhood with a constant pouring that invites you to drift off to sleep under a nice down-feather comforter (granted AC, of course). The soft pitter-patter across the windowpane accompanied by gentle thunder becomes a soothing lullaby for the restless soul. There is no better sleep aid than a thunderstorm.

I used to love rainstorms like that, but not anymore. Not since I realized what it could mean to someone with no shelter from the storm. I remember the rain in Ranger School when I was in the army. Oh, how I hated it. Steel shafts of water pounded my cranium, reminding me that my immortal soul is canvassed with fragile skin and that I'm powerless to protect myself from its wrath. Even in the summer, rain can chill a man to the bone. In the Florida phase of Ranger School, we were each forced to carry a sixty-pound rucksack through the heat and humidity. My uniform was stained white with sweat as I marched through the swamps of Eglin Air Force Base. At night I endured the rain and chills under a holey poncho.

I think this is what's so frustrating about rain. I could control a lot of my situations. If I make the right decisions in other areas of my life, then for the most part, I won't experience pain, but when I'm outside in the elements, the pain comes with the rain.

Relief enveloped me when Brit volunteered to take James back to the streets after SPF7. The entire night, during our Bible study, I glanced at James repeatedly and wondered if someone else would step up. It would have been nearly impossible for me to leave him out in the elements. I gave Brit some money for James, all the while doing battle with the nagging feeling circling in my mind that I could do more. I kept pushing the feeling down, hoping to delay the inevitable action it would require of me. I felt like a kid who doesn't want to take out the trash yet, so he keeps pushing down the garbage with a paper plate.

James climbed into Brit's Nissan Xterra, and they drove toward city hall to find a place that would be James's home in the rain. I watched the red taillights of the Xterra until they turned the corner from Apple Street to Live Oak. I turned the key in my Saturn and flipped my windshield wipers on max.

Traffic was fairly light as I drove north with care on Central Expressway. I exited at Mockingbird, drove north on the frontage road, and turned into the parking lot. I parked the car, grabbed my backpack, and hurried for cover from the rain.

"Hey, Seema." I smiled. "Usual." Seema, who had become my favorite server, moved me to my corner table. She smiled despite looking like she was working the second half of a double. I sat down and pulled out my computer and my Greek homework. This place had become one of my havens. Seema brought me a fruit plate without my asking. The sense of routine brought me comfort. The white noise of the restaurant secluded me, and I moved into a place of focus. I enjoyed Café Brazil. Not only could I get into my zone and work, but I could also choose to be distracted by the college kid with his hair ironed across his face and the skinny jeans that I would never wear in a million years. Or I could listen in on the girl with pink hair explain to her roommate why she thought Mike liked her. Simple distractions made prolonged studying bearable.

As I plugged my computer into the wall, my cell phone vibrated, and Brit's name lit up my LCD.

"What's up, Brit?"

"Bro, I feel horrible. I mean, I just dropped James off at the Laundromat. We're leaving him out there. That's just not right. I hate this, Chris! If I were single, I would take him home and have him stay at my house. There has to be more we can do."

Not only had Brit's speed of articulation morphed from a surfboard to a racecar, but in his passion he said the one thing my soul was crying but had repressed. I wanted him to take it back. I wanted him to reverse what he'd said so that I could continue to put aside what clearly was an affront to my faith in order that there might be no anguish to my soul, but he didn't. He didn't know I was feeling this way, and he also wasn't trying to manipulate my emotions. Maybe it was God who gripped my attention, and now I couldn't turn away.

Brit continued: "Bro, I keep thinking about in the Bible where it says if a dude is poorly clothed and is hungry, and one of you says to them, 'Go in peace, and eat well,' but you don't give them anything, then what good is it? Faith without works is dead, bro.[1] I just feel like our faith doesn't mean anything if we don't help people like this. James is our boy, and I don't know what to do!"

"Yeah," I sighed.

"I left him in a freaking Laundromat. I have a four-bedroom house and a two-car garage."

"I know, man. I live alone in a two-bedroom apartment. I'm starting to feel convicted."

"Bro, sorry—not trying to convict you. I just don't know what to do. But I know we aren't doing enough. I don't want to become the church I criticize."

"Yeah, me either, Brit."

"Hey, I'll see you tomorrow at school; I'm heading home to the wife and am going to study there. Be praying for James. It sounds so lame to even say that."

"Okay. I will. We'll figure this thing out."

"Have fun at Café Brazil."

"Hey, how did you know I was here?"

"Ha, where else would you be?"

We hung up, but the conversation lingered in my mind as I pondered how in the past month my entire worldview had changed and might alter my life forever.

I forced myself to dismiss the thought and focused on Greek. The sky flashed for a moment, and thunder followed on its heels. I looked up from my fruit plate at the rain slapping the glass and sat comfortably in my dry seat, sipping from my coffee mug.

Do not say to your neighbor,
"Come back later; I'll give it tomorrow"—
when you now have it with you.

—from the Book of Proverbs

CHAPTER 7: PRIORITY

I leaned into the glass doors that separated the silence of the library from the hustle and bustle of Dallas. I gave an eye-contact hello to the librarian on duty and headed upstairs to the stacks. Four-inch-thick books on systematic theology sit like sandbags for a student in the trenches of spiritual warfare. Some students wear headphones, while others mouth the Greek words they are trying to memorize. Most academicians choose to follow the dress code of slacks, a collared shirt, and dress shoes, while others, in jeans and flip-flops, make no attempt whatsoever.

I walked past a guy whose beard anyone might confuse with that of Charles Darwin or Karl Marx and headed toward my favorite cubicle near the Gospel commentaries. That was my unofficial spot. I sat down and pulled out my Greek homework and then opened up MySpace and Facebook to see what my friends were up to.

Let's face it: libraries make me sleepy. I had intended to concentrate on Greek, but everything was so quiet and studious. As I situated myself in my corner cubicle, I found my focus more fixed on the inside of my eyelids than on Greek grammar. Even watching the changing status updates of my Facebook friends wasn't keeping me awake.

A couple of naps and a zillion Facebook updates later, I realized I wasn't getting a whole lot accomplished. I figured some company, namely Brit, might help. I like studying with Brit, even though we don't make good study partners, primarily because we don't study. We end up talking about life more than focusing on our respective subjects. But in this case, I decided that spending the time with him would probably accomplish at least an equal amount of productivity. Lately we've been talking about the one thing that had dominated our thinking for the past couple of nights: James.

I packed up my stuff, walked out of the library, and called Brit.

"Hey, man, where you at?"

"Café Koine, bro. Come, join me." The seminary coffee shop—Café Koine—was named after the type of Greek used by the writers of the New Testament. Essentially there are two types of Greek: classical Greek and common Greek. Koine was the common Greek.

I made my way across campus, toting a backpack full of books. Entering Café Koine, I was greeted by Steven Curtis Chapman's "Diving In" over the speaker system. A couple of students sat in plush leather-ish chairs attached to swivel tray tables that held their laptops, folders, and books. Café Koine was less densely populated than the library, which is probably why Brit enjoyed it so much. The fifty-inch TV sat in the corner, forever tuned to ESPN, and Stuart Scott gave us the latest from SportsCenter. At least the seminary had its priorities straight.

Brit had a stack of Hebrew grammar books sitting on the table next to him, but I could tell that he had reached max capacity on brain taxation. Brit wore his Billabong sweater, a collared shirt hidden underneath, a nice pair of black "skinny" jeans that could pass for slacks if you weren't looking too closely, no socks, and a pair of slip-on TOMS shoes that said "Gandhi" over and over and over again across the tops of the shoes. Brit hated the dress code and had no problem expressing his displeasure in it, his staunch stance against it, and his civil disobedience in protest of it. My countless attempts to persuade him about the need for seminary donors to see conservative-looking students so that they wouldn't question that the school's adherence to its conservative theology was understood, but to Brit the dress code served only to distance seminary students from relevancy. I had stopped trying to convince him otherwise months ago. I sat down across from him in my pinstriped slacks, burgundy button-down dress shirt, and black dress shoes.

"You working on Hebrew?" I asked.

"Yeah, you knocking out Greek?" Brit responded.

"Yep."

"You really thinking about James?" he asked.

"Of course."

"Me too."

Brit's world had changed since meeting James and seeing his stark need in contrast to our plush seminary lives. A thought hit me as I attempted to conjugate some Greek verbs. I didn't want to voice it; for to voice the thought would be to admit that I'd had it. And to have the thought would mean that I would have to do something about it or remain haunted by it. As I was about to speak, a woman approached me.

"Chris, I'm sorry to interrupt you, but would you mind signing a couple copies of your book for me."

Brit almost laughed out loud. The woman handed me three copies of the book I'd authored entitled *Faith in the Fog of War*.

"Yes, ma'am, I'd love to," I beamed. "Who should I make them out to?"

"Make the first one to my husband, Bob; he will love your book. The second one make out to my nephew Jason. He is stationed in Iraq. And the third make out to my son Ryan. He is talking about going into the army when he gets out of high school."

"No problem." I zipped through signing the books as fast as I could. "Here you go. I'll see you when the fall semester starts up again."

"Thank you, Chris! My boys will really appreciate it, and this is something they might actually read."

"Ahh. Thanks. Take care."

Brit smirked beneath his Hebrew. My cheeks flushed.

"What?" I said lifting my hands. Brit laughed out loud. I'll be honest; there was certain sense of accomplishment that arose in me when fellow students asked me to sign their books. It was cool. Brit provided a steady balance.

"You're ridiculous, man."

"Why is that?" I smiled.

"C'mon, man; you have people asking for your autograph at school. I'm just praying it doesn't go to your head."

"Thanks for the reminder. It's all about keeping my priority on the Lord. Which reminds me of what I was going say before that woman came." I looked Brit in the eye for a moment and then stared blankly at my Greek. "If I were to do this thing of following Christ for real, no holding back, I would change my priorities."

Brit nodded; his eyes watched carefully.

"These are my priorities," I said. I started to scribble on my Greek homework. "Number one: Dallas Seminary. Number two: speaking engagements to sell books. Number three: my mom. Number four: my dad. Number five: the SPF7 group. Number six: find a wife. Number seven: try not to eat out every meal. Number eight: work out and stay in shape. Number nine: try to publish the next volume of *Faith in the Fog of War*. Number ten: help James."

We both stared at my list.

"You see, behind the worship of God, here is where everything else falls. Notice that it primarily revolves around me. If you were to divvy up my time, James would get all of about 1.2 minutes, and since he gets so little time, probably nothing will change for James unless someone else takes care of it," I said and looked at Brit.

"Well, who's going to?" he asked.

"Trey and Bill are working through their state contacts and the local police departments to get him a new ID card, and if that comes through, he will be set."

"Bro, it's been a couple weeks since then, and nothing has come of it."

"Here's what I've been thinking. What would happen if I put James at the top of the list? What if the largest percentage of my time went to the thing that falls lowest in *my* priorities? What if God's agenda for Jesus is first. What if I am second, and I really thought about others before myself? What if I put James ahead of staring at my Greek homework or studying? Would I be trusting God, or would I be shirking responsibility?

"Hmm. That's deep, bro," Brit responded.

"That's what I think too. I'd better not think about it too long, or I might actually do something about it."

Brit smiled. We went back to studying.

As I went through another Greek syntax worksheet question, a bold urge came over me.

"Brit, I'm going do it."

"Do what?"

"Have him stay with me."

Brit looked at me, trying to see if I had lost my mind. "Have you thought this through?"

"Not really."

"Well, you should pray about it, shouldn't you?" Brit pressed.

"Dude, how much more time do I need to pray about it? James has been coming to SPF7 since early April, and it's now July. You took him to sleep in a Laundromat the other night. If it were you, I would have taken you to my apartment. If it were me, you would take me to your house. Why are we treating James differently?"

"Bro, pray about it. We can't make emotional decisions in the moment that will affect others in the long term. Seriously, pull back the reins and pray about it. You know how I feel about the situation, but I also know how you and me both tackle things with our heart and really don't think it through. Trust me on this. Think about it, and I'll support you."

I let Brit's words sink in. "Okay, maybe I'm being naive. Bill still thinks he's another crack addict looking for a handout, but Bill's so pessimistic, I can't trust that." I sighed. "Maybe now isn't the time, but I want my faith to be more than words."

Praise be to the LORD my Rock,
who trains my hands for war,
my fingers for battle.

—from Psalm 144

CHAPTER 8: WAR STORIES

"Brit, do you mind helping me out with my leadership talk for this weekend," I asked through the phone. I needed someone to listen to my latest talk on leadership that I'd be giving in Colorado for the Night Vision Christian Concert where the Newsboys would be playing the coming weekend. Speaking is how I support myself through seminary, and this would be one of my biggest events yet.

"No problem. Come over, and I'll work on it with you."

I'd worked on the speech for the past couple of days. The Night Vision Concert people had randomly asked me to speak at their venue and were paying me well for it. So the pressure was on to give them something original.

There's not a lot of money in being an author. The term "starving artist" aptly applies. Especially after coming off making captain's pay in the army, the adjustment was quite a pill to swallow.

I arrived at Brit's house and was glad that his wife wasn't there, because I had forgotten to knock. *Married people—different.* I sat down at the table across from Brit, and he eyed me for a moment.

"Bro, this is going to be kinda weird if we stare at each other while you talk for an hour."

"No worries, Brit; I'll pretend there's an audience and talk to them." I got up and started preaching to my imaginary audience. I paused, "Hey, why don't I just share the war stories with you and the lessons I learned. The rest will fall into place."

"Sounds good, man. Whatever you want to do."

"Here I go: I'm former army captain Chris Plekenpol. I commanded Apache Company 2-72 Armor in Iraq. My company team consisted of about a hundred men, twenty-one tanks, seven Bradleys, which are like mini-tanks, a handful of Humvees, and other assorted equipment. My job was to patrol a fifteen-kilometer section of highway that connected Fallujah to Ramadi.

"Every day we were engaged by snipers trying to take our heads off. We were attacked by RPGs (rocket-propelled grenades), sailing over the front slope of the tank, or IEDs (improvised explosive devices), all of which might kill or maim one of my men. Over the course of that year, I lost six men under my command.

"I'll never forget that first day of combat. I was standing outside my command post, watching the heat waves bounce off the minarets of the mosques. I watched the Iraqi people selling ice and groceries. My tanks rolled out into sector. I glanced down at my watch to make sure everything was going according to schedule and 'boom!' A massive explosion erupted about a mile or two out. Smoke and fire billowed into a mushroom cloud about 250 feet high. I went inside my command post and listened to the situation reports coming across the radio. The men were all talking over each other in frantic voices; there was gunfire in the background.

"There are three letters you never want to hear creep across the radio in combat: 'KIA'— killed in action. In the first four minutes, I got the report that I'd lost my first man.

"All of a sudden it feels like the weight of the world is on my shoulders. I grabbed my M-4 carbine rifle and my nine-millimeter pistol and sprinted down to my tank. I mounted the tank and charged my .50-caliber machine gun. My loader took a forty-five-pound, 120-millimeter round and put it into the breach of the main gun; my gunner toggled the switches on the tank's computer, while my driver pushed that seventy-two-ton beast of a machine forty-three miles per hour out toward the West Gate. The emotion of the moment was a combination of two things: the pain of losing my first soldier and the fear that I was about to get into my first firefight.

"As soon as we got into sector, we were greeted by small-arms fire, machine-gun fire, and mortars. I lined up three tanks along the bank of the Euphrates River, and we fired across it to the north at the terrorists. For about fifteen minutes we exchanged gunfire. I sent two tanks across the river to pursue the enemy. I followed in my tank, and about a hundred infantrymen fell in behind me. We started searching house to house to house, looking for any clue as to who or what may have killed my man.

"After seven hours of searching, we found nothing. So at the end of day one, I was physically exhausted from running around in 125-degree heat with fifty pounds of gear; I was emotionally drained, because I just lost my first soldier; and I had to write a letter to his wife, Michaela, and thirteen-year-old daughter, Sara, explaining to them how I let their husband and father die. Spiritually it felt like God had checked out for a while—like he had taken a vacation or a sabbatical and wasn't paying attention, but the lesson I learned from this first day of combat is that you can never let your current circumstances determine your trust in the presence of God."

Brit nodded.

I continued: "That is the first story. Next I'll talk about making mistakes in leadership at West Point."

"Go for it," Brit said.

I gathered my thoughts for a moment and then began: "As a new sophomore and newly promoted cadet corporal at West Point, I had received the authority of absolute power over new cadets. If you are not familiar with the way things go at West Point, a freshman is called a plebe. And the plebe's sole purpose is to learn discipline. He is not to talk outside of his room. He is to obey every legal command that an upperclassman gives him. All West Pointers go through their first year learning the discipline of humbling themselves as part of the leadership laboratory that West Point is. Now, as a nineteen-year-old sophomore having just endured a year of plebe life, it was time for payback. If I wanted an eighteen- to twenty-two-year-old plebe to jump, he would jump. If I wanted him to yell, he would yell. If I wanted him to run, he would run. If I wanted him to tell me the weather, he would tell me the weather; if I wanted him to tell me how many days it was until we had leave, he would tell me. It was required.

"Sometimes, I would be really nice to the plebes and ask a certain one how things were going. Then not an hour later I would absolutely flame him. I enjoyed it. I think some endorphins kicked in, and it gave me a thrill to know that I had that sort of control over another. One day, one of my classmates just stopped talking to me. I could tell something was wrong, so I asked him, 'Bob, do you have a problem with me?' His answer still resonates in my soul. He said, 'You are inconsistent in your leadership; you act like their best friend one moment, and in the next you flame them and make them feel like peons.' In essence, I enjoyed the authority, but I only wanted the responsibility of caring for their hearts when it was convenient. Otherwise they were my little toys to do with as I wished."

"You are a sick S.O.B., man." Brit smiled.

"Yeah, sinful and in need of a Savior," I said. "I'm hoping that I'm not the only sick S.O.B. out there at this festival. I guess that's the point of the story I want these leaders to grasp. I want them to see the way they treat other people through my eyes. There is a tendency in all of us to use power like that, and I think that's why leadership corrupts people. I am titling the sermon 'Leading Servant' to emphasize being a servant over being a leader—okay, next story."

"Hit it," Brit said.

"I'm going to tell a brief story about a soldier coming to me after he had just found out that his wife had cheated on him. That was a hard time. But I think I've told you that one before."

"Whatever you want to do, bro. I'm here for you."

I skipped it. "Okay, another story I'm going to share is that of Cavazos. I recall the day before the battle of Fallujah in November 2004; one of my soldiers, Cavazos, approached me.

"'Sir, uhh—would you pray for me?'

"'Yeah, I'd love to pray with you. Why don't I come down and pray with you later tonight?'

"'Roger, sir.'

"I nodded and returned to him that night. He was on his bunk, and so I pulled him aside and asked him what he wanted to pray about. We walked outside into the ninety-degree November night.

"'Well, sir, tomorrow I'm going to Fallujah. And I don't think I'm coming back. And I don't want to go to hell.' He paused, letting those words hang in the air. 'I know you're a Christian, so if you could pray over me or do whatever it is that you Christians do, I would appreciate it.'

"'Has there ever been a time that you accepted Christ as your Savior?'

"He said, 'Yes, sir, there was one time.' He went on to explain that he had grown up in an abusive family and the struggle that had entailed. He then explained that one night he ended up going to church and heard about Christ and how that gave him hope. But after a series of tragic circumstances, including losing the mother of his daughter, he lived his life to spite God for what he had taken from him. I shared the power of Christ with him. I shared how no matter what he had done, his heavenly Father was waiting and longing for him to come home. His eyes watered, and he just stared at me. He got it. We prayed that night, and he came to understand the impenetrable love of the Savior.

"For several weeks, I prayed for my men in Fallujah. All of Iraq seemed to explode during that battle. My own tank blew up right underneath me. However, we took the city, and all my men who went to Fallujah came back alive.

"When they came back, I found my young private. I asked him, 'How did it go?' He looked down and composed himself. 'Sir, I don't think I'll ever be able to bring myself to talk about it. But amidst all the death and fear, I remembered one fact. Christ is in me as I'm in him, and nothing can separate me from the love of God.'

"He then told me a story that stuck in my head. He said while they were heading into Fallujah, they encountered resistance the whole way. At one point, the tank aborted, which means it broke down. The tank commander looked at Cavazos and told him to get out of the tank and check the engine. Now, being inside the tank is safe, but out of the tank you're exposed. He got out of the tank, went to the back deck, and pulled off the engine plate and went to work. Now there's a certain sound that a bullet makes as it goes past your face. It's kind of between a zip and a crack. So, as bullets skipped in the dirt next to Cavazos, he worked on the engine, and after about twenty minutes of exposure, he dove back into the turret. He told me, 'I never felt closer to my heavenly Father than when I was outside that tank. I knew my God was with me.'"

"Cool story, bro." Brit sat back in his chair comfortably as if I had all night. It was great to be able to practice my talk with a guy who genuinely wanted to hear it.

"Okay, next story—Sergeant Kishbaugh. One day, one of my soldiers was out in sector with his best friend, Sergeant Gibbs. He'd been partnered with Sergeant Gibbs for a while, and they'd become close. Searching the parking lot that day, Sergeant Gibbs came upon a bomb, and it exploded on him. Sergeant Kishbaugh raced to the scene, scooped up Sergeant Gibbs, and tried to save him. Gibbs died back on the base. Sergeant Kishbaugh came to my room frustrated and asked me what this whole thing was about. Why were we fighting? Why did all these people have to die?

"To be honest, I didn't know how to answer him. I sat there for a moment blankly and then said, 'We're here because this world is contaminated by something that causes marriages to end up in divorce and countries to go to war. Sin. Two thousand years ago, Christ came from heaven to earth to pay the penalty for sin so that we could have a right standing with God, which gives him glory, and that is essentially what this whole world is about: giving glory to God by a relationship with him through his Son, Jesus Christ.' Sergeant Kishbaugh just looked at me. 'That is a fairy tale,' he said. 'I can't believe that.'

"'Just because you don't believe it, doesn't mean it's not true. I'll be praying for you.' He excused himself, and I committed to pray for his salvation every day after that. Two weeks later he walked into my office and was just flabbergasted. He leaned against my bookshelf and sighed. 'I just watched *The Passion of the Christ*. If this **** is true, then I'm ****ed. This Jesus **** is pretty ****ing serious. I'm an idiot.'

"It truly was the most beautiful-dirty confession."

Brit laughed. "Dude, are you going to say the actual words?"

"No, man." I smiled. "Don't think church folks could handle that.

"Although he wasn't ready to accept Christ then, later I went to him in his room. 'Are you ready to step over that line of faith?'

"Sergeant Kishbaugh looked past me and said, 'My fear is, what happens if I mess up! What happens if I get drunk? Or what happens if I cuss? I mean, I don't want to piss off God.'

"'Kish, the gospel isn't about making bad people good; it's about making dead people alive.'

"Through tears he came to faith in Christ, so that two months later when he took shrapnel and he had to be evacuated back to the States, he could say, 'I don't know why God is doing this, but I know he has a plan.'"

Brit sipped some coffee and looked at me. "Sounds good, bro. What Scripture are you using?"

"I'm using Matthew 20:20–28—you know, the story about the disciples jockeying for power among the Twelve and then Jesus explaining what true greatness is—it is about being a servant to all. That's why I'm entitling the sermon 'Leading Servant.' That's what I believe we should all be. We need to serve the needs of those around us."

I started to feel uneasy. The reality of what I was preaching might make me a hypocrite. I looked at Brit and said, "If I preach this, then I'm going to have to live this. If I'm going to live this, I must serve James without fear. I must step over that line of fear and just have James come stay with me. You see, I'll never help James until his pain is my own.

"I have to put James as a top priority. I'm supposed to be his servant. The only way that can happen is if I have to stare at his need every day and know it's not going to go away unless I'm active in his world. Christ called us not to be leaders, but servants. I'm going to have to be a servant."

I felt determined. I felt like Trey when he told James the other day that he was going to stand in the gap for him. I knew that what lay ahead wasn't going to be an instant victory; it would be one that would cost me. I wasn't sure how much, but I was tired of my Christian life not costing.

For I was hungry and you gave me something to eat, I was thirsty and you gave me something to drink, I was a stranger and you invited me in.

—from the Gospel of Matthew

CHAPTER 9: INVITATION

I hate to admit this, but that boldness to do the right thing waned over the week. I kept thinking how I was going to ask James to come and live with me, and the more I thought about it, the more I hoped that James wouldn't show up for the next Monday night SPF7. It was kind of like when you make a resolution to go on a diet. You name the date, and in between that time and the current time you practically talk yourself out of it. A part of me hoped that he would never come back to SPF7, and then I could say that at least I put forth the effort and stated publicly that I would look out for him. I kept that thought to myself. I couldn't go to my family for counsel on this, because I already knew they'd think me crazy for even considering it.

I wanted to do the right thing. I wanted to put active feet to my faith. The decision had been made on my part, and I was going through with it. Only James could deter me now.

Monday night came, and so did James. Wearing the same T-shirt and sweats that I had seen him in the week before, he followed Trey into the President's Room. This time he didn't have that homeless smell. However, his attitude still held firmly to that wonderful fragrance—dried urine. His sour demeanor preceded him into the room, and I could feel my heart sink. I wondered how long I could take his attitude in my apartment. It's bad enough during SPF7, but now I was going to invite that bad attitude to take up residence with me.

I didn't immediately mention my decision to have him come stay with me. I had told Brit that I wanted to break the news to him tonight, and Brit kept his lips zipped for me. I didn't want to do it now in front of everyone and possibly feel convicted for waving around my righteousness. So I waited.

SPF7 went with its usual fervor. Tonight truly was a "Safe Place to Fall at 7 PM" for several of the men. The guys shared their struggles from every aspect of life as we encountered God's Word. Some guys shared their frustration with their wives. Others shared about their struggle with lust. Others talked about the need for a job and to get their finances straight. They shared their doubts. Reality and Authenticity shook hands as these men became vulnerable.

My buddy Lance, a classmate from West Point eight years ago, showed up for the first time. I was excited to see him after such a long time. He'd been a hero of mine back at West Point for the way he lived out his faith. He was the president of Officers' Christian

Fellowship while at West Point, and he truly lived out his faith, while I only wanted to.

As the men shared their thoughts and worries, I drifted in and out of the conversation, battling in my mind, trying to find a way to stall the moment of truth—when I would invite a homeless, homosexual, HIV-positive man to stay at my place for the night.

SPF7 came to an end with a round of prayer requests. I sometimes cringed at what James said, because there is a part of me that doesn't want him to talk about how bad his reality is. I didn't want his honesty to scare off Lance or any of the other guys who might be visiting for the first time. But, as I looked around the room, no one seemed annoyed.

"I got robbed last night."

I wasn't sure if I had heard James correctly.

"What?" Trey and Brit asked in unison.

"This skinny, homeless guy came over to me in the middle of the night. He stuck something sharp in my side and told me to empty my pockets. He took everything I had, man. I'm not a fighter. I don't pretend to be. All I had was eight dollars, which may not seem like a lot to you, but it is like a million to me."

That statement felt like an anvil to the chest. James was right. I could lose eight dollars a day and never give it a second thought. I questioned for a moment what James had done with all the money we'd given him, but the question didn't stick in my mind. I just figured he ate three meals a day and after a week of eating out, he had gone through the entire stash of cash. Made sense to me.

James looked down and continued: "I know that I'm a Christian and that God is faithful. But I don't see it. I feel like I'm five steps from walking away from the faith."

"What do you mean?" I asked.

"What I mean is, I know God is faithful, and I know he isn't tempting me, but I feel defeated. I feel alone. I know you guys are helping and all, and it is something to be thankful for, but, fellas, something's gotta give. If it isn't a job one week, it's getting robbed another. The rain hasn't exactly let up, and they won't let me stay in the Laundromat every week. I'm just tired."

Lance stared at me in disbelief. He wasn't annoyed but rather intrigued. James's statement felt like confirmation. I could feel my palms heat up and get a little sweaty. The anticipation caused my body to act like I was in high school asking a girl out for the first time. There was no turning back.

I stared at James and was ashamed of my attitude. I guess I expect too much from people. If only I would look at everyone who is not happy or smiley with a heart that says, "I'm sorry your life is a train wreck at the moment and you don't have the ability to smile." But I always assume they have some unfounded chip on their shoulder so I'd write them off as a bad apple.

SPF7 closed in prayer. I waited for my moment before approaching James. Trey was talking to him, so I prolonged the packing up of my computers and projectors. When James turned to see who would give him a ride back to his corner, I made my move.

"You're staying with me tonight."

A look that can only be described as a cross between shock and disbelief fell over James's face. "Uhh, okay," he mumbled.

I wish I could say that inwardly I felt as confident as I looked outwardly. However, I felt awkward and unsure of my next move. I hadn't quite thought this part through yet. Or perhaps reality had set in, and I didn't want to spend one waking moment with James in my house just yet, or one sleeping moment, for that matter. I'm not sure why. I just didn't.

"Hey, let's go to Café Brazil." I smiled, hoping to further delay a change in my own living conditions.

James shrugged his shoulders.

"Hey, let me join you guys," Lance chimed in.

I was glad that Lance would be there. There was still a little nervousness in me that I couldn't shake. I had my Colt .45 West Point class pistol stationed by my bed with a full clip ready to go. Not sure why I was thinking like that, but I was in new territory. This was something I had never done before, and I wasn't completely sure how the whole thing might turn out. Who knows if James had been snowing me for the past several months? Okay, okay, that is idiotic. I know that, but I'm human and have normal tendencies of fear and assumption that travel alongside making good decisions.

James and I got into the trusty Saturn while Lance hopped into his SUV, and we ventured north once again to Café Brazil. Lance, James, and I sat down and had a huge breakfast at night. Lance and I reminisced momentarily about the days of being cadets, a world that was so far away and in a different dimension now. Lance had a long drive, so after eating, he paid for all three of us and headed home.

James and I stayed until the wee hours. I had this incessant urge to figure out how to get him an ID. Before I knew it, I had spent several hours on the task. I suddenly realized my priority idea had already worked. In an instant I became consumed with righting the wrong. It wasn't for the most altruistic motive, however; it was a self-serving motive. It's a funny thing when a self-serving motive and what God would want result in the same thing. When I find myself doing the thing that serves me is actually the thing that serves God, I know I'm completely in God's will.

I twisted my mind around that thought as I searched the Commonwealth of Virginia database, since James was originally from Virginia Beach, to figure out what the story was on getting an ID and found that you have to have an ID to get an ID—just as James had said. Pretty painful process. Frustration surged as I encountered multiple dead ends. I was on the verge of tossing my computer through the window until it hit me how hard this has been for James.

Crud.

How many other men were out on the streets because the bureaucracy of the system had worn them down? I didn't know. Don't hear me say that the system is wrong. I don't want just anyone to have access to an ID only to pull off a terrorist attack under some pseudonym, but there has to be some other way. I searched and searched until I realized that James's stay at my place would stretch more than a week.

"Ready to go?" I asked James.

"Go where?" he asked.

"Home."

James paused, which always made me wonder what he was thinking. "What's up, James? Do you want to go somewhere else?"

He nodded. "Yeah, I was gonna do laundry tonight. Can we do this tomorrow?"

"Sure," I said, trying not to look relieved.

James and I went out the door into the humid Dallas night. We got into my gray Saturn and headed back toward the ghetto. We made a turn on Grand and another turn onto a dark street. I felt slightly uneasy.

"Stop under the light," James said.

I stopped under the light.

"I don't want you driving in an unlit area in this part of town," he paused and looked around.

"Plus down here, people could think I'm playing with the cops." Great.

"I'll pick you up tomorrow night at eleven, on your corner," I said.

"Okay, I'll see you then."

I pulled out and headed back to my apartment. It was around four o'clock in the morning, late enough for the traffic lights to rest for the night and simply flash. Bright splashes of red and yellow pulsed across my windshield. I felt like the lone patron of an outdoor disco. I kept driving, all the while wondering why James decided to do laundry in the middle of the night. I also wondered about this oddity of dropping James off in a place where people would worry about cops. I let that thought go; who knows why people do random things? Maybe James was feeling me out and was just as nervous about me as I was about him.

I pulled into my driveway and went up to my apartment, savoring my last night of freedom. *God loves a cheerful giver*, the words from 2 Corinthians echoed in my mind. If I couldn't get a better attitude about this endeavor, my attempt at righteousness—and any help I hoped to offer James—would lose its value to the Lord. That sounds so churchy, but I really believe that. I want my life to be about something more than just me.

God, change my heart, I prayed. *Make me want to want to do this.*

Then they will call to me but I will not answer;
they will look for me but will not find me.

—from the Book of Proverbs

CHAPTER 10: MISSED

I was out on a date on Tuesday, so I told James I would be there to pick him up after that. After I dropped off my date at her house, I headed over to the corner of St. Paul and Corsicana. Brit called. "Bro, I just saw you with your date!" He laughed. "How did it go?"

"It went pretty good," I responded.

"Where's James?" he asked.

"I'm heading over there now. I told him I would pick him up about this time."

"Let me know how it goes."

I followed St. Paul all the way until it hit Corsicana. Homeless men littered the sidewalk. Some slept; some argued; some stared at me. I rolled along at a snail's pace, trying to ascertain whether

James was somewhere in the midst of this cheerless throng. From my vantage point on the other side of the road, no one looked familiar. I wondered if he might be at the library, so I pulled away from "the corner" and crept back in that direction. The streets teemed with homeless people. I had not driven this part of town late at night, ever. And if you don't have a reason to—don't. Some men appeared to be strung out on drugs. They ranted at transgressors visible only to themselves. A chorus of rage filled the night. It was interesting but eerie. I didn't see any women. I wondered for a moment why that was, and then I pushed that thought out of my head. I dared not imagine the fate of a woman trying to survive in this environment. That might be sexist, but in a world where strength and dominance rule the day, women just don't fare as well.

James wasn't at the library. I headed back to "the corner" to look for him again. This time, I stopped the car, rolled down the window, and examined each individual resting on the pavement. I was probably the only white guy in a four-block radius. I know I must have looked like a cop or someone suspicious because, really, how many young white guys come driving around "the corner" and stare at the homeless? A skinny black man was thinking along the same lines and stood up. He took a few steps toward my car, lifted his hands in the air, and gave me the "What's up, punk?" look. I started to calculate the time it would take for him to walk to my car and the time for me to spot James without confrontation.

I decided that maybe tonight wasn't the night. I left the skinny man shouting behind me. I wondered what had happened to James, but in all reality, I wasn't prepared to go toe-to-toe with the entire homeless population of Dallas to find out. I knew if I got into an altercation that I would soon be surrounded by about a hundred men. Odds were not in my favor. I would fight another day.

I called Brit.

"Hey, man, I can't find James."

"Did you check by the Day Resource Center?" Brit asked.

"Yep."

"Did you check by the library?"

"Yep."

"Did you go to the corner of Corsicana and St. Paul?"

"Yep," I said.

"Is anyone out there?" he asked.

"Yeah, there are tons of people, but I haven't seen James anywhere."

"Hmmm . . ." Brit thought out loud. "Do you think he's avoiding you?"

"I don't think so. Maybe he is having a hard time receiving help?" I asked.

"I don't know. Why don't you come over here and study with me. Ash is away, and I'm just doing homework."

"On my way."

I got to Brit's minutes later, and he and I did Hebrew and Greek for a while with our usual efficiency. Our conversation hovered around James again.

"Man, it has been eye opening hanging out with James. I really needed this, Chris. I really did. James has given me so much to think about with faith and God and what it all means. Last week he and I went to dinner, and we really talked. He shared about his life on the street and his struggle for holiness. Honestly, it blew me away. His life is so simple, and we make it all so complicated."

"I know. I think it's awesome that you have really connected with James like that. SPF7 has become really close and really special through all this. We have a common cause to unite around. I wonder what would happen if more Bible studies adopted a homeless man. Think of how we could turn this city around."

"Great thought—look, man, we've got to study or else I'll never make it through Hebrew this summer."

We went back to work as best we could, stopping ourselves when brilliant ideas of how to change the world trickled through a solid defense of Greek and Hebrew. Finally, I got tired.

"Hey, man, I'm done for the night. I'll see you mañana."

"Okay, man." Brit picked up his phone and put it to his ear. I thought it odd that he would be checking his messages then, but I just paused and waited to give him the official backslap-goodbye hug. Brit lifted his index finger indicating for me to give him a minute. He progressed through several messages that I couldn't hear, but the last message on his voice mail had been left by a particularly loud talker.

"Hi, this is Nurse Hansen from Baylor Hospital. James wanted me to call you because he could not get a hold of Chris to let him know that he is in the hospital. James had a mild heart attack and came in." Brit moved the phone toward me so I could hear, but he didn't need to; I already could hear her loud and clear.

"What do you think?" Brit asked.

"Well, I guess he's at the hospital. She gave us a call-back number. What time did she leave that message?"

"Oh, wow, five this afternoon."

"It's after midnight now, almost one o'clock. I can call the number tomorrow. I'm sure James is staying there tonight. If he calls you, just let me know, and I can go pick him up."

"Okay. I wonder if he's all right." Brit's concern was apparent, and I realized that I should be more worried than I was.

"I have no idea. How can we know?"

"We can't," Brit said.

"What else can we do?" I asked.

"Nothing right now—I'll let you know when he calls."

I left Brit's house and made the fifteen-minute drive back to my place. I was spared once again from having James stay with me, but I realized that my heart was still more worried about the inconvenience to me rather than his well-being.

I wondered what caused the heart attack. My mind swirled with possibilities. I pulled into my gated driveway, got out of my gray Saturn, unlocked the apartment door, and walked up the lonely stairway to my humble abode. Flipping on the light, I noticed that the place was strangely clean. It startled me for a moment, and then I remembered I'd actually cleaned my apartment in preparation for James coming tonight. I had a conversation with the Lord asking him to bless James in whatever was going on and let me be in tune with his will and respond in love to the situation with James at all times.

God would have to change my heart about him staying with me or this whole thing wasn't going to work.

Let their lying lips be silenced,
for with pride and contempt
they speak arrogantly against the righteous.

—from Psalm 31

CHAPTER 11: Call

The next day came with the challenge of cramming forty-eight hours of stuff into a twenty-four-hour day. It was six o'clock before I knew it, and the day had escaped. I finally called the hospital number the nurse had left, but it must have been after everyone was gone for the day, because I got the "nobody is here" message. I left a voice mail, unsure if anyone would let James know I was concerned. I didn't receive any calls. The next day passed. No news.

Brit called on Thursday.

"Hey, bro, James called me."

"Really, what did he say? Where's he been?"

"He said he was there when you drove up to the corner."

"What?" I tried to remember back to that night and wondered if I'd had an irrational fear or if it was the subconscious underpinning of not wanting James to spend the night that kept me from seeing him there. I then wondered, as an Airborne Ranger combat veteran, if I was allowed to be afraid and, as an outspoken follower of Christ, if I was allowed not to search high and low when I didn't find him.

"Yeah, bro, he said that the hospital had released him, and he went to wait for you at whatever time you guys had agreed to. He fell asleep and was sleeping whenever you drove by."

"What was I supposed to do? Walk up to every guy with a hood over his face, peel it away, shine a flashlight in his eyes, and check? I mean, c'mon."

I was starting to get exasperated. James knew I came to get him and now was complaining that I didn't see him when he was asleep!

"Brit, I mean seriously, that is ridiculous! What did he expect me to do?"

"Whoa, slow down, bro. Your beef isn't with me. Check it out; I explained to him that you looked for him, but the situation was starting to get dangerous. You can work this out with him this weekend or something. Take him to coffee or dinner or something."

"I'm going to Colorado to speak at that Christian festival, followed by a trip to speak in Missouri on Sunday and then back to Dallas on Monday for class. I guess the next time I'll see James is on Monday night at SPF7."

"Don't worry about it, bro; you'll work it out. Focus on your weekend. James will be here when you get back."

"All right, man. Later." I hung up and frustration immediately seized my shoulders. James was supposed to be grateful. Yet, he wasn't showing it. Okay, maybe I hadn't looked hard enough. Maybe I did get spooked for no reason. Maybe I should have gotten out of the car and looked at each sleeping man. I don't know. It seemed kind of ridiculous for him to be upset. But then, I hadn't been homeless for the past couple of years. I didn't have to worry about what I was going to eat or wear, not because I had faith, but because I had food, clothing, and enough money to live on. My whole life has been filled with much, and his has been filled with false promises and broken hopes and dreams. Was he starting to see me as another broken dream?

Truth from God's Word spoke to my heart. *In Christ we too have been claimed as God's own possession, since we were predestined according to the one purpose of him who accomplishes all things according to the counsel of his will.*[1]

God is sovereign. As a believer in Christ, I know that I have to trust that God is working this out. But that doesn't mean that things aren't going to be difficult. Getting involved in people's lives is messy.

Why didn't James just talk to me? Why was James talking bad about me? I mean, what's the point? I tried to calm down and focus on the fact that these difficulties might be a part of God ordering my steps to receive disappointment or to gain compassion. This isn't just about James. This is about me growing in Christ and being a minister of his love. Christ received rejection and loved anyway. God's refinement included frustration for me but would ultimately lead to my deeper walk with him.

I also knew that these events may have occurred for James to gain perspective and put his trust in God as opposed to people. His trust in people and in his ability to flee from drugs or the homosexual lifestyle may have been what crippled him from letting the

Holy Spirit work in him. I don't know. All I know is that God has a purpose for this situation and that it may be for his glory and my suffering, which in the end would be for my good. It may be for God's glory and James's suffering. It may be to make the story a little more dramatic, so that more people read about how God providentially showed himself to be true and good through the lives of a couple of men. I don't know. I just know that God is in control. But I also know that I'm not happy.

I gave Bill a call.

"Hey, guy, what are you doing?"

"Just getting ready to go to Colorado. What are you up to?" I asked.

"Just lusting after some Harleys on my favorite road-trip website."

"I'm frustrated, man. James is upset because I didn't see him when I went to pick him up from the street corner."

"Man, this guy is playing you," Bill retorted.

"We don't know that," I shot back. "Have you found out anything about getting his ID?" I asked, changing the subject.

"Nah, nothing yet. Trey is getting all of his stuff packed up to go, and my contacts are having a hard time getting back to me. But I'm tellin' you, man, something just don't feel right about James."

"Bill, he may be droopy, but he's a good guy."

"I'm glad you think so, guy. Look, just be careful."

I hung up with Bill and realized that his sympathy wasn't exactly the kind I was looking for. I was frustrated, but I couldn't let that frustration taint my view of James, or else I ran the risk of feeling resentful about having him live with me. I knew that would be the toughest part about inviting him over to my place. I'd better prepare myself now or inevitably pay the price later.

Each man should give what he has decided in his heart to give, not reluctantly or under compulsion, for God loves a cheerful giver.

—from the Second Letter to the Corinthians

CHAPTER 12: inside

The much-anticipated weekend started with a flight to Grand Junction, Colorado, speaking at the Christian festival, and then driving 250 miles through the night to Denver. I hung out at a Denver coffee shop for an hour before the airport opened and then made my flight to St. Louis, followed by a 150-mile drive to Lebanon, Missouri. I spoke at another Christian festival, went to the hotel, wrote a Greek paper, then drove back to the airport in St. Louis, and boarded a plane to Dallas.

Before we landed at DFW, I went into the lavatory. Washing my hands, I glanced up and noticed the puffy bags and the red lining of my eyes. *Glamorous.*

My flight got me back in Dallas just in time for Greek class. I headed home as fast as I could, picked up my Greek textbook, and drove toward the seminary. Greek didn't stop for speaking engagements.

On the way I called Bill to check on things back on the home front. He told me he had actually taken James to lunch and was starting to doubt himself. He wouldn't go as far as saying he trusted James, but at least Bill attempted to see in him what I saw in him. I appreciated that.

I had to suck up the tiredness and drive on through the pain of a class I wasn't into that day. I hoped my professor didn't notice me analyzing the second hand of the clock more closely than the paradigm he was trying to explain. He soon dismissed us, and I slouched home and passed out on the couch. I woke up a couple of hours later with enough time to eat some canned chicken, get dressed, and make my way back to the seminary for SPF7.

As I drove to the seminary, dread weighted down my shoulders as I wondered how James would arrive. I assumed I'd get his I'm-doing-you-a-favor fish handshake and a droopy face that I wanted to slap.

Brit meandered through the door as I set up the room. Holding a venti Starbucks coffee and a piece of pizza, James followed him. His fallen face looked blankly past me. I would have to start all over again in this process of loving James well. But *to God be the glory, to God be the glory,* I kept thinking, trying to convince myself. I watched to see if the chip on James's shoulder would fall off; I remembered last week's confrontation. One of the other members of SPF7 had shared his sin struggle, specifically explaining before he began, "I don't want any advice; I just want the struggles I'm facing to be heard." So when James started to chime in with some wisdom, I shut him down.

"James," I said, "this isn't the time. Our brother here said he didn't want advice tonight. We're here to listen."

James looked down.

Brit told me later that in James's mind every time he spoke I was out to get him. The not-picking-James-up-on-the-street-corner fiasco didn't help matters. He told Brit that he felt I had something against him. Brit had attempted to quiet his discontent by reminding him that it was the group moderator's job to ensure that everyone was heard and that he should not take it personally when I corrected him.

We went through the Bible study, and tears were shed again as the heartaches of life continued to flow. One of the guys flat out said he hated his wife and felt trapped in a lifeless marriage. Another one of the guys inspired all the rest of us toward sexual purity. He was married and was having trouble with his wife because she wasn't as interested in sex as he was. To show his love for her, he fasted from sex for forty days. No sex. No masturbation. No nothing. It is possible. He slept in the same bed with his wife and continued to love her but resisted the temptation to "satisfy himself." It wasn't out of legalism but rather from a heart of love. He made it. His marriage has blossomed as a result, and the men in our Bible study now live by the fast that goes by his name.

SPF7 ended, and I edged up to James. "Hey, man, you stayin' with me tonight?"

He looked up with only his eyes at first, as if in disbelief. "Okay."

I wasn't sure if he was irritated or truly shocked. I wondered if I came off as a jerk at some point, but I decided to ignore his apathetic attitude and be excited. "Come on, man. This will be fun."

He followed me gingerly as we walked to my gray Saturn in the parking lot. I thought about taking another trip to Café Brazil to put off the inevitable, but I felt that if I didn't just take James home, he might slip through my fingers again. My pulse quickened as we went to my house. I pushed the remote for the driveway gate. It opened slowly, and I secretly prayed that the landlords weren't anywhere nearby. They're not Christians, and I don't think they'd understand if they saw a homeless guy trouncing through their yard and into the guesthouse I rented from them.

To further exacerbate the issue, my car had been broken into the morning of my first Barnes & Noble book signing. I didn't want them thinking that I was bringing in homeless guys for insurance payoffs.

Hoping to avoid a confrontation that might totally blow any chance I had to help James, I decided to keep him on the DL—the down-low. As if a modern-day Corrie ten Boom, I quickly entered the driveway with precision and speed, parked the car, exited the vehicle, and moved James up the stairway into my apartment and closed the blinds. Success.

I laid down the ground rules as best as I could. James could have any food in my house he wanted, which to be honest wasn't much. He would sleep in the master bedroom, which I had converted into a living room, and he could go anywhere in the apartment except my room—that was off limits. I had a king-sized air mattress, which worked very well, and he would sleep on that. I told him he could shower as often as he wanted. I limited him by flatly stating he wasn't allowed in my house alone until I built up more trust for him. I just wasn't ready for that yet. Therefore he would get up with me at six thirty, leave the house with me at about seven, and I would drop him off at the Day Resource Center or the D.A.R.E. Center or anywhere he wanted to go. At the end of the day, I would pick him up around ten o'clock.

At first he was a little resistant to the rules and acted like he was about to jump ship on the whole thing.

"Hey, man, if you don't trust me, don't let me stay here."

"Dude, it isn't that I don't trust you, but I'm trying to put proper boundaries in place so that I don't resent having you here. The last thing you would want is for me to feel like you are a burden. This is how I can cheerfully serve you, and it will be my pleasure."

That seemed to make sense to James.

I then started on my Greek homework. There was a moment when I wasn't sure if I should talk to James or just work and let him be. After sitting at my dinner table and staring at my computer for several minutes, I decided that we should pray and let God sort out all of the awkwardness. I knew this was big. I knew this was a chance to make a difference in James's life and, more than likely, a huge difference in my own life. I knew that I would be stretched over the next couple of weeks to months or however long it would take to get James on his feet. I just hoped and prayed it would be closer to the former than the latter.

I sauntered to James's room and gingerly opened the door. "James, do you mind if we pray before we go to sleep?"

James knew the value of prayer and agreed. I asked God to give us both patience as we learned what it was to live together. I asked the Lord to take two separate cultures and mesh them together under the head of Christ, reminiscent of Ephesians 2:14–15.[1] I prayed that God would remove any barriers between us and that we would have open communication to discuss the good, the bad, and the ugly. God help us. James in turn prayed that God would bless me in every way, especially financially. And that in turn, I could bless James. I thought that was pretty cool.

We said amen, and I headed back to my room to pray alone. God help me. For a moment I wondered how much I didn't have a clue about. I wondered what my family and close relatives would think if they knew. Then I decided not to care. This is living! This is the gospel, and as I wrapped my mind around that thought, I felt a surge of power run through my soul, as I understood that we were, in a small, small way, pushing back the darkness of Satan's grip.

Give to the one who asks you, and do not turn away from the one who wants to borrow from you.

—from the Gospel of Matthew

CHAPTER 13: MORNING

Beep, Beep!! I awoke with the usual jolt of my overly loud alarm clock I had placed in the next room to ensure I would get out of my loft bed. The jolt caused me to bang my head against the ceiling once again. You would think that I would get used to the fact that I slept less than fifteen inches from the ceiling and that I could never actually sit up in bed. I had to "combat roll" every morning from my loft bed to start the day. Sometimes, I would miss the ladder and crumple to the floor. However it did economize my space.

After knocking myself awake, I rotated my body out of the loft bed and safely down the ladder. I sauntered into my bathroom with a little more pep than usual to start the morning ritual. James was still asleep. I brushed my teeth and listened to the cheesy Christian radio station that I never turned off. I always liked the reminder of hope when I was home alone and more so in the presence of some homeless guy. I glanced in the direction of James's room and wondered what God had in store. Was it really possible for one person to care enough to actually change things for another?

I spit in the sink and wiped my mouth with the back of my left hand. I got dressed and went to James's room and slowly opened the door. James slept in the fetal position, clutching his bag. I nudged him on the foot with my shoe. He woke up and immediately put his hands over his face as if someone had clubbed him in the noggin. He was still groggy, and for a moment my mind went back to Iraq when I used to wake up my lieutenants for the weekly combat meeting. I would kick open their door and sing, "Rise and shine and give God the glory, glory. . . ." My lieutenants would look back at me the same way James looked at me now; only this time I wasn't singing.

I looked at my watch. I wanted to leave by seven o'clock to get to the school by seven thirty for my Greek study group. I watched James for a moment to make sure he would get up. James was moving like pond water, and I tapped my watch for him. He mumbled to me that he wouldn't shower this morning. Rolling over onto his hands and knees, he pushed himself up. He picked up his hygiene kit and made his way to the bathroom. I stared at my watch, while he brushed his teeth and relieved himself. He came back to get his stuff ready to go and looked for a moment like he would take his blankets and other things.

"You can leave that here," I said. "You're staying here tonight."

James looked at me for a moment, shrugged his shoulders, and put some things into a day bag that he'd tote around till evening.

We went downstairs to my car and got in quickly enough so that my landlords wouldn't know I had a homeless guy living with me. I really dreaded the thought that they would find out, because I knew beyond a shadow of a doubt that James staying anywhere on the property would go over like a lead balloon.

We drove downtown to the Day Resource Center. As I was about to drop James off, he said, "I'm hungry."

I wasn't sure if that was a question, demand, or observation. It reminded me of an old girlfriend who made statements like that all the time. I eventually learned that those statements were really manipulative demands. My stomach started to churn as I felt an invisible hand creeping over the pocket of my wallet.

Scripture started to pound against my head again, and the book of James began to trickle out of my soul, *"For judgment will be merciless to one who has shown no mercy; mercy triumphs over judgment. What use is it, my brethren, if someone says he has faith but he has no works? Can that faith save him? If a brother or sister is without clothing and in need of daily food, and one of you says to them, 'Go in peace, be warmed and be filled,' and yet you do not give them what is necessary for their body, what use is that? Even so faith, if it has no works, is dead, being by itself."*[1] I pulled out a ten-dollar bill, and trying as hard as I could not to have an attitude about the deal, I placed it in his hand.

"James, I can't do this every day. I don't have a job other than speaking. Even then, I'm not paid that much. I hope you understand."

James acted offended. "I don't want your money. I was just makin' a statement." *Ahh, there she was again.*

The awkward turtle sat in my lap for a moment. I grabbed James's hand and firmly placed the ten-dollar bill there.

"Take it, man. Get something to eat," I said sheepishly.

I pulled up to the gate of the chain-link fence that led into the Day Resource Center. Homeless men milled about. I stopped the car and hit the unlock button, which made a loud click, letting James know the door was open. He got out and crossed the dimensional portal back to his own world. Before he shut the door, he poked his head back in the car and said, "What time are you pickin' me up?"

"Ten o'clock tonight."

James drooped and said, "I'll see you here."

He shut the door limply, and I wondered for a moment if it was even closed, but I decided to drive on without checking. I sighed and pressed on the gas toward the seminary. Something in me did not sit right. James expected me to serve him. I pushed the thought away and reminded myself that I was supposed to be his *freakin'* servant and that it was my *joy* and *privilege* to serve him. I drove to school and plastered a smile on my face.

Dr. Grant, one of my seminary professors, always says, "You'll know when you have a servant's heart when you start to get treated like one."

"I can do this," I said out loud to myself. "That wasn't *that* hard. I mean, I guess all that is required is that I do it for one more day."

I prayed that this wouldn't be as big a sacrifice as I expected.

Defend the cause of the weak and fatherless;
maintain the rights of the poor and oppressed.

—from Psalm 82

CHAPTER 14: IDENTIFICATION

My theory of one day at a time was working. It didn't seem like a terrible burden having James in my apartment. In fact, I almost enjoyed having someone else there, especially at night. I felt like we were a team, and when I dropped him off in the morning, I no longer felt obligated to give him ten bucks. I rather enjoyed providing for him. There was an odd sense of fatherly pride that came with taking care of someone to give him a hand up. The week passed with relative ease. My comfort and trust level with James began to rise.

Toward the end of the week, I started to feel a new sense of urgency to get James an ID. On our first Friday morning together, I didn't know how to accomplish this, but I knew the first thing I could do was start trying. I wanted to go to city hall with him to see if my presence could make a difference in getting him an ID. Pastor Richard Ellis of Reunion Church Dallas had given me a call and told me that if I merely go to city hall and stand with James in line, it would probably be enough to get him an ID. I was willing to try anything, so I told James to meet me at the library at one o'clock that afternoon, and we would go together across the street to fight city hall.

This was my first attempt at social justice, and, to be honest, it felt good. I knew James was homeless, but he had had a stint of bad luck. I mean, all he needed was a little grace, and I wanted to be that guy to deliver that grace.

It was 12:45 PM, and I was running behind on sending a couple of copies of *Faith in the Fog of War* to a TV station in Florida. I called Brit to see if he wouldn't mind picking James up and meeting me there. He agreed and said that he would call me when he had James.

As I left FedEx Kinko's, I answered my vibrating phone. It was Brit.

"Hey, bro, where is James supposed to be again?"

I gave Brit the location as I headed to my car. I thought I might be able to beat them there with some divine aid because, as you know, everything between men is a competition. I maneuvered to city hall and found a parking spot that had more than an hour of time left on the meter. *Ha! Victory!* I thought. *Things are going my way.*

I called Brit. "Where are you, man?"

"Bro, I can't find him. Where did he say he would be?"

"He should be at the corner of Young and Ervay," I replied. "That's right in front of the library. You can't miss it."

I started to walk from city hall to the library. I wondered if something had happened to James. Did he get hurt? Did he not care? What happened?

Brit called me. "Bro, he's nowhere to be found. Where you at? Oh . . . I see you . . . pink dress shirt. Bye."

I motioned to Brit on the sidewalk, and he pulled over.

Brit started, "Hey, bro, I gotta jet. I have a thing with my wife."

"No problem. I totally understand. Where do you think he is?"

"Not sure," Brit answered.

"Hmmm . . ." I said aloud. My mind started to work overtime. I wondered if he had been beaten up or if he had fallen into drugs or alcohol. I wondered what the deal was. James had looked fine. He always had, but for some reason, doubt was creeping into my head. I pushed the thought away—with force this time.

I decided to go inside to the DMV and find out if what James had said about how to get an ID was true. Besides, I needed to update my address on my own ID card from my mom's house out in the suburbs to my Dallas residence. Because I moved so much in the army, I just kept my mom's address as my home of record. That, of course, was very beneficial as Texas has no state income tax. I love Texas.

As I entered the broad doors of city hall, I shouldered past several citizens who were also tending to their identification issues. For a moment I thought I might see James among the throngs. I noticed a part of me didn't want to see him right now. I couldn't place the feeling or figure out why all of a sudden I wasn't up to being a Good Samaritan.

Everything changed when I got inside. Something about realizing I had to ask for help intimidated me. I don't want to be a burden. I also don't like asking for directions, since the locals never know where anything is anyway. Maybe that's part of my man DNA.

I followed the signs to the identification-issuance place. I dreaded waiting in line and trying to figure out how I would bring up wanting to help a homeless guy. It gave me flashbacks to childhood.

My family moved a lot when I was a kid, and friendships came and went. Whenever we moved anywhere, my mom would sit me down in front of the phone and wouldn't let me leave until I located a friend to play with. That was my mom's remedy for an only child's boredom. Standing in line I could feel myself staring at those numbers on the phone and trying to think of what to say to a kid I didn't really know. I'm not sure what the issue was then, but I guess I didn't like feeling vulnerable or needing someone.

Besides, I was in summer school, for crying out loud—studying the elements of Greek—so there. I have better things to do. At least I had my own reason to be here, for my own ID, a good cover.

I asked the security officer posted at the DMV line how I could help a homeless person. I explained the situation as best as I could muster. The look on his face was a mixture of annoyance and rejection.

"Sir," the officer started, "the person you are helping has to have three forms of ID. He needs to have the army DD214 form. He needs a voter registration and perhaps a school transcript or a Social Security card."

James hadn't lied. I thanked the officer and made my way to the clerk to get my address righted on my driver's license. The clerk made some comment about how I could have done this online, and I did my best to let it go and moved out smartly.

Where was James?

"Bring the whole tithe into the storehouse, that there may be food in my house. Test me in this," says the Lord Almighty, "and see if I will not throw open the floodgates of heaven and pour out so much blessing that you will not have room enough for it."

—from the Book of Malachi

CHAPTER 15: Silver

I picked up James as usual that night around eleven from the DRC. He looked at me like I was crazy when I told him about hanging out at the DMV and waiting for him earlier that day. James somehow thought it was next Friday. I don't have the best memory, but I could have sworn that we'd agreed on that morning. I decided to drop it and never thought about it again.

He told me that he had spent the day at the library, doing a word study on holiness. James is not a seminary student, but he did go to Bible college. I asked him if he had parsed Greek and Hebrew verbs in the process, and he said no, but he had gotten out a library concordance and looked up all the different places the word *holiness* appears.

James's problem had been that he could not get past his homosexuality and just be straight. He kept telling us that he couldn't be straight, but he could be holy. All he had to do was find out exactly what that meant and how to do it. It was a noble task, but one that I didn't think would come with study. I think that one comes with applying what you do know and asking the Holy Spirit to give you the strength to do it.

The weekend passed uneventfully. We hung out at the library, Starbucks, church, and restaurants. James wasn't a cheap date.

My mood switched again, and dread returned as I thought about taking James down to the DRC on Monday morning. The more he stayed with me, the more difficult it became to watch him daily return to the streets. But what else could I do? Leaving him at my house all day would do nothing to change his situation. He didn't need another day off. He needed to actively pursue work. Watching him slump away with five or ten bucks started to wear on me. My prayers focused on God providing. I'd also decided to blog about the situation and had been continuously mentioning the fact that I was praying that God would provide.

Okay, God, let's do that open-up-the-window-of-heaven deal and pour out some blessing.

I hoped the blog might glorify God somehow—that the world would see that people really can change.

In response to my blog, a guy with the MySpace name Silver Spoon wrote me a message.

Would you allow me to financially help James? My contribution wouldn't be substantial, but nonetheless, something.

That was it. I sent him a MySpace message back and told him that we meet at the seminary once a week on Monday nights and that if he ever wanted to come and check it out, he could. I gave him the address of the seminary and didn't really think that much about it when I didn't hear back from him.

The next day I went to the library with the plan of working on some Greek. Sitting in the reference section, I realized I needed a book behind the circulation desk before I could start the process of knocking out one of my Greek papers. *Let me tell you, Greek is exhilarating.*

I approached the library clerk as fast as I could, hoping to beat the guy who had just entered the library and was also making a beeline for the circulation desk. He beat me. I tried not to look frustrated and stared at my library card in my palm not to appear upset.

"Ma'am, I'm looking for a student here. His name is Christopher . . . Christopher K." The man leaned over the circulation desk as if her computer monitor had his answer.

The library clerk paused, not knowing exactly what to say to that. I waited patiently, wanting to crawl into a hole for her. The library clerk looked at me apologetically. Then the man looked at me. I acted like I hadn't been staring at him and wondering what in the world he was doing, but then he went from looking at me to staring at me.

"You're him! You're him!"

I looked at the library clerk, pleading my case that I never knew this man. I quickly placed my ID on the counter. "I'm Chris Plekenpol. Not Chris K." He then looked at me and said, "MySpace."

My jaw hit the floor. It was Silver Spoon. I directed him outside the library so we didn't have to use our inside voices.

As soon as we got out of the silent chamber, he looked at me. "How is James? Where is James?"

"He's probably at the city library, the Day Resource Center, or the D.A.R.E. Center. He'll be at SPF7 tonight if you'd like to come."

"I can't make it tonight," he responded. "But you have to keep telling the story. I want to help James out. I didn't know how I'd find you, but I drove out here from Fort Worth. I believe in what you're doing, and I want to be a part of it in some way. It isn't much, but here is fifty bucks." He padded my palm with a fifty-dollar bill. I couldn't believe it.

"Man, this is a God thing. I was actually kind of worried about finances. I've wanted to give James more money, but I'm a seminary student, starving author-speaker guy, trying to make ends meet; what can I do? And here you make a huge difference. Praise God for you."

We hugged and he turned to leave. I went back into the library and stared through the window at the man as he got into his car and drove off. My thoughts couldn't return to Greek.

Every now and then I'm confronted by God. Every now and then I realize that life is not about me but is instead about the story God is writing through me. I turned around, half expecting to see Jesus transfigured. A surreal feeling tingled my skin. I can't explain *feeling* close to God. You just know when you are. It's like touching time. It's like smelling color. It's like hearing infinity.

Those moments when God intervenes and lets me know he's watching don't come every day. They serve as reminders that he wants me to live by faith. But that is so difficult because I want to see results. I want to see life change, and when that doesn't happen, I get frustrated.

This thought hit me. I don't serve James because of James; I serve James because of God. So James's actions don't matter. If James never gets on his feet and I do an exercise in futility, it doesn't matter, because my God told me to always remember the poor. So here I am doing it. Here I am living this thing called faith. Fifty bucks is not the mother load but a shadow of what is at God's disposal if I can trust him. God's sovereign power and my working out my salvation with fear and trembling work in tandem. I'm still trying to figure that out—that God already knows how this story will end, yet he allows me to make active choices to play a part in his plan, yielding my soul to his Spirit so that I may be conformed to the image of his Son. I don't understand God. I'm glad that I don't. It makes a surprise fifty dollars all the more exciting when I don't understand it, don't analyze it, but just accept it.

That night I took that fifty dollars and presented it to James at the Bible study. A weird hush fell over the fifteen men present. They looked at James. They looked at me. They looked at the fifty dollars. As I handed the cash to James, I wondered what his thoughts were on this whole thing. I was afraid to ask him. I didn't want a droopy response to ruin my God moment.

Then some soldiers asked him, "And what should we do?"
He replied, "Don't extort money and don't accuse people
falsely—be content with your pay."

—from the Gospel of Luke

CHAPTER 16: HMMM?

James had asked me earlier in the week if he could stay at a friend's house to do some laundry. I wondered how big James's clothes collection was and why he never just brought it all over to my house to do laundry at the Laundromat with me. Maybe spending too many nights sleeping at the Laundromat made him want a change of scenery. I always hoped that he might be giving some encouragement about what God was doing in his life to whomever it was that he stayed with for a night or two. So I left it at that.

The next night James didn't come home. I wondered if he was trying to make a career out of doing his own laundry.

My cell phone vibrated. I smiled as I lifted the phone to my ear. It was Bill.

"Hey, guy. Got some interesting information." Bill was a little more straightforward than usual, which made me nervous. There were times I wish he wasn't so to the point, but mostly I really appreciated it.

"What's up?" I asked.

"Trey and I made some phone calls today. James wasn't fired from the Melrose. I called down there, and they said he'd worked there and that he did a good job but that he just quit showing up one day."

"Didn't James say something about that?" I asked.

"Not that I know of. There may be more to this than you think. I know you think the best of everybody, but I've seen guys on drugs for the past thirteen years. He may be using you as a meal ticket. I'd bet on it."

Bill wasn't new to this scene. If there was a man who had seen it all, it was Bill. I think that's why we became so close so fast. I had seen a lot of blown-up people in Iraq, and he had seen the most bizarre things on the streets of Dallas in his job on the Narcotics Task Force. Two of Bill's stories always stick out to me.

In 1989, Bill was on one of his first patrols in the southernmost part of Dallas County. He saw a vehicle parked in a remote area with its lights off. It hadn't been there earlier, and it looked suspicious. He turned off his squad car's lights and carefully crept up on the vehicle.

As he got out of his patrol car, he could hear someone saying something from inside the vehicle. He approached the vehicle with his partner, and they both put their flashlights on it. Inside they observed what turned out to be two naked people.

They started scrambling for their clothes. Bill ordered them out of the vehicle naked and told them he'd get their clothes for them. That kept the possibility very low of one of them going for a weapon, which, at the time, was standard operating procedure. The two exited the vehicle, and Bill was shocked to find a thirteen-year-old Hispanic boy and a twenty-four-year-old Hispanic female.

The kid was wide eyed and afraid. The female however was used to the game. Bill could tell she was once a beautiful woman, but the years of heroin addiction and prostitution had worn her body down. Her arms were covered with fresh and old track marks, one of which had begun to abscess.

Bill handed them their clothes and began to question them. They both spoke Spanish and claimed not to speak English. That was no problem for Bill, who is fluent in Spanish. He got the details of the incident; the most frightening was the fact that they didn't use condoms. She was the neighborhood prostitute, and he was just a local kid. She'd been a prostitute since she was fifteen years old. Her uncle and father had been her first sexual experiences. She escaped the abuse and found help from a pimp who got her addicted to heroin.

She was arrested that night for having sex with a minor and transported to jail. Bill took the kid home and told his parents. The father seemed to be unconcerned, while the mother was visibly upset. Once Bill mentioned that no condoms were used and that she was a heroin addict with fresh track marks, the father realized his son was in real trouble. This was especially dangerous since it was at the beginning of the AIDS scare.

That was Bill's first experience with depravity, but he would soon see more and far worse in his years on the force.

Another memorable story was the time Bill kicked in the front door of a house in response to a child screaming. He moved to the far back bedroom and encountered a man with a three-year-old boy. The man turned out to be the boy's uncle, who was supposed to be baby-sitting him. The uncle had been abusing the boy for some time.

Bill recalled later that he secretly wished the uncle had given him more of a reason to send him to his Maker for an early meeting.

However, despite Bill's experience with those involved in drugs and living the hard life, I didn't want to think of James in that way. That couldn't be him. There had to be more of an explanation. I was conflicted and decided that the only thing that would put my mind at ease would be to confront James and ask him directly about it.

"Thanks for the warning, Bill. Please keep checking to see what you can find out."

"No problem."

"Oh, hey, one more thing; have you given up on trying to get James an ID?"

"That ain't working, and that's not the real issue here. We can't keep enabling him, especially if he ain't legit," Bill said.

We hung up, and I let my mind rattle around the possibilities. *Was James really on drugs and snowing me? Was Bill looking to avenge a vendetta from his past? God, you've got to help me out here.* I pushed these thoughts from my head. Homeless people get a bad rap I convinced myself. James was fine. I knew his story would add up if

I simply asked him. Besides, he was never drunk or high. He always looked and smelled fine. Well, except for a little B.O. from not showering. But other than that, he was fine.

A couple of hours later my cell phone rang.

"This is Chris."

"This is James. I'm ready when you are to come back and stay with you. You gonna come get me tonight?"

"Yeah, I'll be at the DRC at eleven o'clock."

"Can you make it the library? I'll be out on the bench outside if that's cool."

"Okay, see you there at eleven."

I continued to work on my Greek till quarter to eleven, then packed up my homework, and left the seminary library. I made my way downtown, rolled up to the library, and looked around. I didn't see anyone. I put my car in neutral and put on the parking break. The street was deserted. Nobody was out there.

Knock! Knock! A black fist pounded against my window, startling me. My heart raced for a moment as adrenaline shot through my system. It only took me a second to realize it was James, but I'd already instinctively put the car in first and released the parking brake, ready to race off. *The fight-or-flight response still works.*

I unlocked my car door. James got inside and slumped into the seat, investigating the small chips in my windshield.

After my heart moved back down into my chest, I looked at James, whose gaze was firmly fixed on the windshield.

"Hey, man," I started, "what happened when you worked for the Melrose?"

James looked at me, offended for the moment. He was probably wondering where this was coming from, but I decided I would let the question sit on his shoulders.

"I couldn't get to the job, so I stopped going."

"Why couldn't you get there?"

"I got stabbed."

"Oh."

That was all I needed to hear. I had forgotten that life on the streets meant there was a good chance you could get robbed. It meant that you had to watch your back. Getting robbed or hurt by another person on the street wasn't something I've ever thought about. My own naiveté was embarrassing, and for a moment I regretted asking the question. I felt at ease about James and his situation and resented Bill's suspicion and constant negativity toward James.

I drove into the driveway, satisfied and tired. James got out gingerly and followed me up the stairs. We prayed together briefly before bed. As I got up from my knees and was heading back to my room, I paused at the door frame.

"Hey, man, feel free to take a shower. That's what it's here for. Remember, mi casa es su casa."

"Okay."

No more questions from me. I walked into my room, climbed into my loft bed, and stared at the ceiling. The newness of James had worn off for everyone else. No one told me anymore how awesome I was for taking James in. James was now simply my roommate, but I wasn't yet completely comfortable with having him there. He smelled and wouldn't take a shower. My hints at the shower had not quite been taken in yet. He was always droopy and negative. I knew that soon we would have an argument or a conflict that would really test my commitment to James. Before I went to sleep, I prayed for continued wisdom with this man and that I wouldn't grow weary of doing good.

I knew I was doing the right thing. I was no longer doing James a favor. I was just learning to live with a stinky roommate. The giddy feeling of doing something right and good was being replaced by the realization that this wasn't a quick fix. If I were going to live a sacrificial life for Christ, an actual sacrifice would have to be made.

Even though my illness was a trial to you, you did not treat me with contempt or scorn. Instead, you welcomed me as if I were an angel of God, as if I were Christ Jesus himself.

—from the Letter to the Galatians

CHAPTER 17: SPOT

I turned the corner of Cadiz and slowed down in front of the Day Resource Center. I looked for James. A crowd of homeless men and a few women mingled on the sidewalk. If I hadn't done this so many times before, I would have been intimidated. I spotted him sitting against the chain-link fence. He smiled. I mumbled a prayer of thanks that, for once, his face didn't droop and that he appeared grateful to see me. At least it seemed that way.

Click.

James had grown accustomed to the wordless invitation of my doors unlocking. He pulled the car door open, and as he did, he sneezed. He then reached across the car and shook my hand. I wiped my hand on my pant leg.

"Bless you," I said.

"Thanks."

"Any work today?" I asked.

"No. Nothing."

As we drove toward Starbucks, my thoughts turned to James's health. It concerned me that he had been sneezy almost every time I picked him up. At any given moment, his nose lingered on the brink of a snotty eruption. "James, how long have you had that runny nose?"

"I don't know; I guess it's allergies or somethin'. It's just always runnin'. I don't think it's somethin' you can catch."

I wondered how long it would take for me to catch whatever James had. He wiped his nose again with his forefinger and thumb. He wiped his pants. I wiped mine too, out of habit. I know HIV is not an easy disease to catch. I certainly had no plans to share needles, have sexual contact, or become "blood brothers" with James. But despite what I knew to be true about HIV transmission, as I looked at James's snotty hands, I couldn't help but wonder if that virus was virulent or dormant somewhere on his slimy fingers. Sure, HIV is a fragile virus that can't survive long outside the body, but perhaps James's particular virus could be defying the odds amid a handful of mucus that protected it from the deadly air.

My overly analytical mind ran the statistics on that and deemed the ability of mucus to hold HIV alive and transmit it through my skin as highly improbable. However, the opposing forces of fact and fear were lining up to wage a nightlong battle in my mind. I couldn't wait to get to Starbucks and wash my hands. I planned to stay there tonight as long as possible because, well, although he's been staying with me for a week or so, it's just kind of weird hanging out with a gay homeless man alone in my apartment.

At Starbucks, James read one of my books that was required reading for my introduction to theology class. Jack Deere's *Surprised by the Voice of God* was about how the gifts of the Holy Spirit are alive today and to deny them is to merely be a Bible deist—I just hoped James wasn't getting inspired to "lay hands on me." I watched him wipe his nose with his dirty fingers and then wipe his pants. He put his hands on my book and then on the table. Glancing at the people around me, I couldn't help but wonder if my bringing James here had been an irresponsible decision. It seemed as though he was touching everything. I prayed briefly for the air to kill the virus, all the while chiding myself for being so irrational. I tried without success not to obsess about it, but HIV was my only thought.

"Hey, man, you ready?"

"Yeah, that's cool," James snorted.

We got in the car, and he sneezed again. I had stopped saying, "Bless you," about ten sneezes ago. That didn't stop him from sneezing. I could feel myself almost getting angry at the man for not caring that he might be contaminating me. I kept my thoughts to myself.

When we arrived at my apartment, we went upstairs and got on our knees to pray. I asked the Lord to bless James's health as well as mine.

"All right, man, I'm tired. I'll see you in the morning. Same bat time, same bat channel."

"Yep, I know, six o'clock."

"Night." I went to sleep thinking of floating HIV, and I awoke with a cold. As I went about the daily process of getting ready, I realized my voice was a little hoarse. For a speaker, dealing with a hoarse voice is one of the most wretched things imaginable. If you can't talk, you can't change the world. If you can't change the world, you might as well crawl into a hole and die. Okay, a little extreme, but when I get sick, I start thinking like that.

This might sound ridiculous. But I realized that there is something special about being sick. I was connecting and relating with James on a completely new, deeper level. It is difficult to minister to someone without sharing his struggle—without sharing in his sickness.

Romans 12:9–16 ran through my mind. I thought that my sharing in James's troubles could be how I'm learning what it is to be like Christ in how I love people. *"Let love be without hypocrisy. Abhor what is evil; cling to what is good. Be devoted to one another in brotherly love; give preference to one another in honor; not lagging behind in diligence, fervent in spirit, serving the Lord; rejoicing in hope, persevering in tribulation, devoted to prayer, contributing to the needs of the saints, practicing hospitality. Bless those who persecute you; bless and do not curse. Rejoice with those who rejoice, and weep with those who weep. Be of the same mind toward one another; do not be haughty in mind, but associate with the lowly. Do not be wise in your own estimation"* (NASB).

Okay, let's be real here. I don't want to share in James's sickness. The previous evening I had to force myself to shake his hand without making a face. I don't want HIV. It doesn't matter how informed I am on the transmission of the disease. I've seen the pictures of what happens to HIV victims once the medication stops working, and my basic human reaction is to run as far from that as possible. But truthfully, I didn't even want to share the man's case of the common cold. Slimy hands gross me out. However, my ability to share in his cold allows me to see life more from his vantage point and empathize better and feel what he feels as opposed to standing over James trying to get him to pull himself up by his bootstraps when he doesn't even feel like moving.

I don't want to be Mr. Preacher guy here, but I guess being like Christ requires that I share in James's hardship so that I may give him hope. More Scripture flooded my head, as if the Holy Spirit knew what I needed to hear. I thought of when Jesus explained to his disciples that whenever they fed the hungry, they did the same for Christ. Whenever they invited in the sick, they did that to Christ. You can't heal a sick person without being exposed to the sickness. That thought sat heavily on my chest.

Matthew 25:35–40 says, *"For I was hungry, and you gave Me something to eat; I was thirsty, and you gave Me something to drink; I was a stranger, and you invited Me in; naked, and you clothed Me; I was sick, and you visited Me; I was in prison, and you came to Me." Then the righteous will answer Him, "Lord, when did we see You hungry, and feed You, or thirsty, and give You something to drink? And when did we see You a stranger, and invite You in, or naked, and clothe You? When did we see You sick, or in prison, and come to You?" The King will answer and say to them, "Truly I say to you, to the extent that you did it to one of these brothers of Mine, even the least of them, you did it to Me"* (NASB).

Was I really serving Christ through my service to James? What if I wasn't fully excited to do it, yet? Did it still count? I was beginning to see that the motive does sometimes follow the action.

I had forced myself to spend time with a contagious (with a cold, that is) James the night before because I knew it was the right thing to do. In his grace, God had accepted that nominal offering and gave me a deeper understanding of what it is to live on the streets constantly trying to keep an immune system going that is exposed to repeated attacks. This grew in me a softer heart toward James and a greater compassion for those on the streets.

God had opened my eyes to truth I had never experienced before. This is what it is to give back to the One who redeemed my soul. What a shame that it had taken me this long to figure out what all those verses meant. But to be honest, they had never been applied to my life. I usually skipped over them.

Do nothing out of selfish ambition or vain conceit, but in humility consider others better than yourselves.

—from the Letter to the Philippians

CHAPTER 18: 4:00 AM

The last time I dropped him off at the DRC James told me that he would call me when he was ready to come home. He had laundry to do again, and I didn't have a washing machine or dryer. He had once again made arrangements to do laundry for a night or two at one of his friends' house.

I hadn't heard from him in a day or so, and I was getting a little worried. It wasn't often that James said he would be somewhere and then not show or call. I knew he could take care of himself, but still, there was a part of me that wondered where he was. I told myself to quit it and not to play the role of a nagging mother. James was a big boy and was probably fine. At forty-five years old he could take care of himself, so I had nothing to fear. At least, that's what I thought.

My phone rang. I didn't recognize the number, and something immediately told me this was James. I picked it up.

"This is Chris," I answered.

"This is James," came a calm voice. I was relieved. "I'm in the hospital."

"What? What happened?" I interjected. "Are you okay?"

"Yeah, I should be okay. They're needin' to run some tests. I think I might be here for a while."

"Tell me when you're going to get out, and I'll come and get you," I said.

James hesitated. "That might be a while," he said. "I don't want to bother you."

"Brother, anytime. I told you I was here to stand in the gap for you. I don't care what time it is. I'll be there." I heard the words coming out of my mouth, and for a moment, I wanted them back. I mean, I wanted to do the right thing, but maybe this was going a little overboard.

"Okay, thanks," came the reply. "I'll call you later."

I hung up the phone relieved and a little worried. What if James died? At least the SPF7 group would have been a part of his last days. Other crazy thoughts flitted through my head, and I wondered how this whole thing might play out.

I went about the rest of my day, but I couldn't shake the nagging anxiety that I might miss James's call. Several times I caught myself staring at my cell phone, waiting for it to ring. A part of me wanted him to call now so I could pick him up and go to bed. Another part of me hoped he wouldn't call until tomorrow. The cold he'd given me a couple of days prior was setting in, and my voice was completely gone. I was tired and a little upset too.

Why do I have to be the one to pick James up? Where is Brit or Bill or Trey or someone else? Can I get any help here?

Then I remembered that I volunteered to do this. It was my own words that had put me in this situation. No one else told me to do this. No one else expected me to do this. Well, almost no one. I got that feeling that God was watching and nudging me to abandon my role as guest of honor at the pity party.

It was eleven o'clock at night, and I honestly wanted to turn my phone off. Okay, I'll admit it. I turned my phone off. I reasoned that I was sick, and after coughing up phlegm a couple of times and taking another Halls, I headed for bed. But then my conscience couldn't bear it, so I turned my phone on again. I wondered what would happen if I just left my cell phone in the other room on vibrate. Would it be my fault if I didn't hear the phone? The victim in me made his case.

Why don't you get some sleep? You're tired. James can take of himself. He was doing it long before he met you.

But that pesky Scripture started to cry out once again. *Therefore, to one who knows the right thing to do and does not do it, to him it is sin.*[1] How strange that the Scripture I recalled tended to come from the book of James. Was this a coincidence? Or was God purposely making it impossible for me to abandon James, my sullen, contagious houseguest? Either way, God's Word was clear. There was no way I could let him down. I would answer James's phone call.

I got out of bed, grabbed my cell phone, and crawled back under the covers. I issued a brief prayer that I wouldn't have to get up earlier than seven and drifted off to sleep.

At four o'clock, I was awakened by something vibrating on my chest. Startled, I sat up too quickly and banged my head against the ceiling—ah, the loft bed. After recovering from the blow, I answered the phone.

"Hello," I said in the most groggy, sick voice possible.

"I'm done," he said simply, implying that now it was my turn to do something.

"Okay. I'm on my way," I said without hesitation. I hung up the phone and fell back asleep. I know what you're thinking. How could I tell him that I was going down there and then totally go back to sleep? You win. I'm a terrible person. But don't worry; God intervened. He wouldn't let me sleep. I awoke fifteen minutes later almost wide awake. I crawled down the ladder out of my loft bed, found a T-shirt, some shorts, and flip-flops and stumbled down the stairs to my car.

As my key turned in the ignition, things started to come back into focus. I started driving the two miles from my house to the hospital. *How many times in the future am I going to be doing this?* I didn't want to start a pattern here. But as I was driving, that weird feeling of "right" trickled into my soul. I found myself smiling. In fact, I was downright happy. At the time, I didn't think to question the source of that happiness. I just accepted it.

I pulled into the emergency room drop-off area and saw James sitting on an outside hospital wall. He didn't look thrilled, but then, he rarely did. I stopped and unlocked my doors.

James got in and slumped into the seat. He didn't look at me but rather stared straight ahead into the windshield.

"How are you feeling, man?" I asked with genuine concern.

"Like crap," came the real answer.

"I'm sorry, man. What's wrong?"

"They don't know. I may have had a light heart attack. They ran a lot of tests and gave me some medication."

I decided not to push it. "I'm glad you're okay, man."

"Thanks."

We drove home in silence, pulling in the driveway as the clock on my dash turned to four thirty. We got out of the car and went upstairs.

"Good night, James. Hey, church is at eleven thirty, man; sleep in." I smiled at that thought.

Suppose one of you had a servant plowing or looking after the sheep. Would he say to the servant when he comes in from the field, "Come along now and sit down to eat"? Would he not rather say, "Prepare my supper, get yourself ready and wait on me while I eat and drink; after that you may eat and drink"? Would he thank the servant because he did what he was told to do? So you also, when you have done everything you were told to do, should say, "We're unworthy servants; we have only done our duty."

—from the Gospel of Luke

CHAPTER 19: GRATITUDE

The next morning I woke up at nine o'clock and was unable to go back to sleep. I decided that as long as I was up, I might as well get to work on my Greek paper. A little groggy, I slowly went about the task of translating. I listened to the stunted rumble in the next room, which I could only imagine was the sinus congestion giving James fits in his sleep. The snoring subsided for a moment, and I looked at the door to see if James might join the living.

He appeared from his bedroom on a mission for the bathroom. The sound of the toilet flushing preceded his appearance in the dining room. He slumped down in a chair at the table across from me and stared in my direction. At first I wasn't sure if he was looking at me or through me. It looked like he wanted to say something, so I closed my Greek text and gave him my attention.

As if on cue, James mumbled, "I got somethin' to say."

I felt my heart sink, and I'm not sure why. I think anytime anyone has something to say, I automatically get a negative vibe. It might be a programmed response from when my mom used to tell me, "We need to talk," and then I had to endure a lecture. I looked, intently waiting for James's next words.

"I don't know how to say this. And I've been told that I don't say this well," James started and paused.

Say it already!

James looked at the table and said, "I've been told that I'm not very good at saying thanks. I never have been. I'm a man who at times doesn't know how to express myself. I just want you to know that I'm thankful for everything you've done for me."

I tried to capture James's eyes. He never looked at me once during his whole monologue. I wondered why this was so hard for him to say. But regardless, I was grateful.

"Thanks for saying that, James. I'll level with you; I was wondering if anything I was doing mattered to you. I love being in your life, and I believe that God is working through you. I feel like God is really teaching me how to serve without looking for anything in return. And, dude, I mean that. I really want to serve you."

"Thanks."

We sat in silence for a moment.

"Man, I want to be the guy that God uses as a catalyst in your great story. You know, I'm blogging this thing on the Internet and telling about how you are going to make it. God is going to use you in a big way."

"Okay," he said.

I was hoping for a more enthusiastic response, but whenever I said words like that to James, they fell flat. It was as if the thought of him being great or God using him in the lives of others could only happen in another dimension. Frankly, I shouldn't be surprised. It had just dawned on him that my helping him might be a burden and that I was going out of my way to make things better for him. He'd never thought of saying, "Thanks," before.

My spirit lifted.

In general, it helps when the person receiving the assistance acknowledges you are going the extra mile. It made me think of my parents and how I never really told them thanks for taking care of me. That's just what parents do. They picked me up from school, basketball practice, and any other extracurricular activity. They made sure that I had every necessity to succeed in school as well as what I deemed essential—like Air Jordans. They also put inside me a real sense of *I can do anything*. I love that.

So, here I am, thirty, and this guy is forty-five, and I'm taking care of him. It took me picking him up at four o'clock in the morning for him to say thanks. I guess I owe Mom and Dad a thank-you.

I had an epiphany. James's confession was no surprise—anyone at SPF7 could have told him—James has an issue with gratefulness. However, it sparked for me a clear view of my own deficiency. The issues I see in others illuminate my own sin. The only reason I can see them in others is because I recognize them in me as well. I can't become more like Christ if I never get a picture of what I really look like, no matter how distorted the image. That awareness changes me. It furthers my spiritual growth and also allows me to give more grace to those with whom I share the same struggles. This takes me back to Jesus and his Sermon on the Mount.

"Do not judge so that you will not be judged. For by the standard you judge you will be judged, and the measure you use will be the measure you receive. Why do you see the speck in your brother's eye, but fail to see the beam of wood in your own? Or how can you say to your brother, 'Let me remove the speck from your eye,' while there is a beam in your own? You hypocrite! First remove the beam from your own eye, and then you can see clearly to remove the speck from your brother's eye." [1]

So, *that's why* Jesus said that, because my tendency is to think of myself as perfect and everyone else as flawed. I would have never believed I was ungrateful for anything, but sitting across from James, it dawned on me. We were not that different. He just knew it, and I just realized it.

While those thoughts flashed across my mind, we didn't say a word. James stared at the wall. I looked at James. What was said was enough.

"Hey, man, take a shower. We're going to church in a bit, and not to be rude, but you could use it. I'll take one after."

"Okay," James answered.

We each got ready and talked a little bit about nothing at all, then headed off to church. I was glad James was okay, and I was glad I got to pick him up from the hospital at four in the morning. As we drove to church, I wondered how many more times God would call on me to sacrifice like this.

Good will come to him who is generous and lends freely,
who conducts his affairs with justice. . . .

He has scattered abroad his gifts to the poor,
his righteousness endures forever;
his horn will be lifted high in honor.

—from Psalm 112

CHAPTER 20: COMMITMENT

"Hey, Brit, over here." I motioned as he walked into Café Koine. He'd called earlier that morning, saying he wanted to talk.

He smiled, walked over, plopped some books on the floor, and sat down across from me. He hadn't trimmed his long sideburns in a while and was starting to look Eddie Munster-ish. I studied his face for a moment. He was only twenty-seven, but deep lines grooved his forehead. It seemed strange that a man who spoke in a surfer dialect would have such heavy worries, but it could be that he was one of those deep-thinker types. He reminded me of Rodin's *The Thinker*, that French statue with the guy sitting down, hunched over with his fist under his chin, all deep in thought. I wondered why he wanted to talk to me.

"Hey, bro."

"What's up?" I asked.

Brit's cool demeanor hid the fact that he grew up poor with a single mom near Houston. His fortunes had improved with time. He graduated from Texas A&M, and I imagined that if the ministry thing didn't work out, as long as he stayed in Texas, the networking power of the Aggies would be a great fallback. No matter what financial circumstances he faced, I was certain that he would always be a guy who never forgot where he came from.

Brit's eyes drew me in. "Ashley and I've decided something," he said.

I was hoping they wouldn't decide anything. Brit had talked about moving, and that was probably what he was going to say, so I braced myself.

"Bro, we're going start giving fifty bucks a month to James. I budgeted it out, and if we cut out a coffee here or there, we can do it."

I relaxed. While I'm a fly-by-the-seat-of-my-pants kind of guy, Brit and Ashley manage their finances down to the penny. He even mentored several other seminary students and taught them how to budget their money to graduate from school debt free. He made labeled money envelopes covering every conceivable expense from A to Z to include necessities as well as some luxuries like Starbucks. He didn't have a credit card, and everyone he counseled cut his or hers up.

"That's awesome," I said. "I definitely need the help."

"No problem."

"Hey, what all do you give to?" I asked innocently.

Brit looked at me quizzically for a moment and then shrugged his shoulders. He looked around to make sure that he wouldn't be overheard and lowered his voice.

"We support a couple Indonesian missionaries who are fighting the sex trade. I can't wait till next summer to go over and work with them and get some sweet surfing in. The waves out there are outrageous."

"I love how you're reaching out."

"I've known them for a while—good people."

"Do you support anyone else?"

"Yeah, Ash and I recently met a teenage chick who is living a hard life near Texas A&M. We're helping her get a college education. We might have her move in with us next summer so she has a place to stay while she works to raise money for school."

"Wow, anyone else?"

"Yeah, but I don't want to go into all that right now. Just wanted to let you know that Ash and I really want to support James in a big way and see his transformation all the way through. We had James over for dinner the other night, and he really gave Ash and me a new perspective about life. I mean, here I'm a seminary student and I'm learning, bro. I'm learning from him. I think there is more to this than any of us really get. I believe in him, bro. I really do. I know Bill thinks you're crazy, and sometimes I do too, but if we're going to do this, we might as well do it all the way.

I was amazed at their generosity. "Thanks, man. It's good to hear that. Sometimes I feel crazy. Like I'm out on an island. That's a huge relief, man."

"Good, bro."

"How do you want to handle this? Do you want me to give him the money, or are you going give it to him directly?"

"I think we'll give it to him directly. That way James isn't always asking you for money. We know you are struggling. Ashley is doing awesome at her job, so this is something that we have been praying about to expand our ministry. Bro, I wish we made more, so that we could give more. But this'll have to do for now."

"Brit, I think you're on to something."

"I don't know, bro; I just want to be faithful with what I've been given."

"So do I."

"Thanks. I'm actually meeting James for lunch downtown. Gotta jet. Just wanted to let you know the deal before I told him. And seriously—I mean this. If you're ever feeling overwhelmed with all this, let me know, and I'll be there for you. Call you later."

"See you, Brit," I said.

Brit waved and walked toward the door. I called after him. "Hey, Brit!" He looked over his shoulder briefly. "Thanks."

"That's what the church does, bro. See you."

Wow, crud. I thought my efforts of giving a homeless guy a place to stay and get back on his feet were something to be proud of, and I had been giving him ten bucks every time I had cash on hand. Brit budgets out every penny he has and gives it to the cause of Christ around the world and in his own city. I'm going to do that—eventually.

If I start thinking about that too much, conviction will rain down on me, and I'll have to sit down and evaluate my money and make real decisions about the mini-luxuries I take in, like Starbucks. *Do I have Starbucks five times a month or have the chance to save a little girl from being sold into the sex trade at two years old?*

Seriously. I'm going to stop thinking about that right now.

116

When times are good, be happy;
but when times are bad, consider:

God has made the one
as well as the other.

—from the Book of Ecclesiastes

CHAPTER 21: SUPERMAN

It was early evening on a Wednesday night. I went to pick up James from downtown. My friend Christina from church and her friend Amanda, who was visiting from Los Angeles, were in the car. Amanda, who had been following James's story on the Internet, had flown in to DFW to visit Christina earlier that day. James didn't know my intentions for the evening, and I liked it that way. When he got into the car, Amanda turned and handed a small gift bag to him.

"I thought you might need this," she said.

He accepted it and immediately opened the present. I couldn't help but sneak a peak at the gift. *A wallet? What does he need that for?*

James opened the wallet and then shut it real quick. I leaned over covertly as he looked at it again. Five twenties lined the inside of the wallet. My eyes went wide for a moment as I watched out of the corner of my eye. *Who was this girl?* She had read about James from MySpace and Facebook, but she didn't know him. God is bigger than my expectation.

Driving from downtown Dallas to Arlington, I could see James's eyes wonder where in the world we were headed. About a month before, he had told me offhandedly that he'd wanted to go to the Six Flags Over Texas amusement park and ride the roller coasters. He recounted several stories as if Jesus himself lived there. I figured, *What the heck, you only live once.*

As we pulled into the vicinity of Six Flags, James's eyes looked like headlights with the brights on. "Are we going where I think we're going?"

The rest of us smiled.

"Oh my God, oh my God! I've been waiting, I don't know how long, to do this. I knew you would come through, Chris. I knew you would!"

"We all came through, James," I said, trying to be humble.

We got out of the car, and the four of us walked up to the ticket booth. It's summertime here so the park is open until eleven. I had my trusty season pass and was hoping that it could work some magic in getting a lower ticket for the four of us since there were only a few hours left until the park closed. No one was at the ticket booth. I walked up to the ticket taker and informed her of the problem.

She looked at me. She looked at my friends in tow. She looked at me, and then—she waved us through. "No charge. Go ahead."

"Okay," I said and whisked my friends through before she could change her mind.

Thanks, God, I smiled inwardly.

We immediately went to Superman, followed by the Titan, followed by Batman, Mr. Freeze, and then Flashback. We screamed a lot. We laughed a lot. We ate ice cream. For a moment there was no homelessness—just four friends having fun.

The whole time James jabbered about how much fun he was having. It was like watching a ten-year-old on his first trip ever to Six Flags. The whole time I felt as if a little light shone in the darkness. Hope had arrived. If God could get us into Six Flags for free, could he not get James a job and get him on his feet?

As the park closed, we headed out the gate with a wave to our ticket taker, who was now sweeping up around the entrance turnstiles. We got into Christina's SUV and headed back to Dallas. James's eyes were slightly glassed over.

"This has been the greatest night of my life. Y'all made a difference. I feel like a real person with real friends. Thank you for doing this for me."

I smiled. I made the mental note that this was the second time for James to say thanks. So this was particularly huge. I decided not to look a gift horse in the mouth and enjoy the blessing.

On the way home James made a strange request. "Can you drop me off downtown? I'm gonna stay with a friend and do some laundry."

"James, you know you can stay with me. I can drop you off to do laundry in the morning."

James's face wrinkled for a moment. "No, that's okay. I don't want to burden you. I have to store my laundry somewhere, and it's too far to walk from the Laundromat to the DRC in the heat."

"I have a speaking thing tomorrow night at the Frontiers of Flight Museum that's probably gonna go late. I'll have to pick you up after, probably about eleven," I said.

"That's fine."

"You sure?"

"Yeah, it's cool, man."

I thought for a moment. James couldn't bring his stuff into my house during the day because he would be seen and the landlord would ask a ton of questions. I decided that James probably knew what he was doing. So I told Christina to take James back to his part of town.

She followed James's instructions to a part of Dallas where everyone knows nothing good ever happens. We passed a shopping cart parked in the middle of the road in front of a dilapidated house that looked like it was one beam away from collapse. The girls looked wide eyed as we drove through the area.

"Stop right here—under the light," James said. "I want you to be safe."

Christina stopped under the light. There were six African-American men probably in their early twenties wandering around. It was about midnight, so we appreciated the light since all eyes locked on us like we were the Klan. I watched James take his day bag and march up the hill to what I was now thinking might be a . . . I stopped the thought.

I had dropped him off here before and just didn't think anything of it. But could this be a crack house? *Nah*, I thought. James is too smart for that. Besides, everything is going so well; why would he want to screw it up? He looked fine. He wasn't on drugs. So most likely, he was okay. *Right?*

I pushed the thought away, and Christina drove me home. I unlocked the door and walked up the stairs into my apartment. I paused by James's room and then went inside it. I looked through his bag of papers briefly. His Bible was there with a stack of admittances to the hospital as well as some health records. There were some magazines for those who are HIV positive. I put the bag down and felt like I was being intrusive. I could trust James. He wouldn't do anything to deliberately ruin our trust. I know what Bill said, but there would be no reason for James to throw it all away.

I went into my room and got ready for bed. As I closed my eyes, I smiled. *At least I won't have to drive James to the DRC in the morning.*

Restore to me the joy of your salvation
and grant me a willing spirit, to sustain me.

Then I will teach transgressors your ways,
and sinners will turn back to you.

—from Psalm 51

CHAPTER 22: TEENAGERS

The next night, after my speaking engagement, I hurried over to pick James up from the DRC. He wasn't thrilled that it was eleven fifteen, since I'd told him I would be there at eleven. We rode in silence back to my apartment. James didn't smell quite as bad. Guess he got a good shower and actually did some laundry. *It'd be nice if he washed his attitude.*

We walked up the stairs and into the house like old roommates. We briefly prayed together and then went to bed.

The next morning James showered without prompting, and we made it out of the house earlier than I had ever thought possible. I dropped him off at the DRC and was early to my Greek study group.

I picked him up again that night, and we went to hang out at Starbucks. I blogged James's story for a while, and he continued to read about the power of the Holy Spirit. I think he was actually excited that I was writing his story, documenting how God was transforming his life.

"You want anything to drink?" James asked.

"You buyin'?"

"Yeah, I think I owe you," he said.

"Cool, man. I'll have a café white mocha."

"You got it."

We didn't talk much while sipping our coffee. He read and I wrote, and the night passed effortlessly for once. Around ten, we headed home, prayed, and went to sleep.

Saturday morning, we headed off to the DRC around seven. "James, I'm going drop you off, and I'll pick you up late tonight."

"What're you gonna do?"

Why does James have to be so nosey? I thought about lying, but that whole West Point brainwashing thing prevented it. I couldn't lie, cheat, or steal if my life depended on it. I was going to Six Flags with Kevin, one of the kids I mentor, and I wasn't sure I wanted to tell James, since he might want to go as well. And it wasn't like I didn't want James to go, but this was supposed to be my time with Kevin.

"I'm going to Six Flags," I said without emotion.

"Can I go?" came the immediate response before I could even exhale my next breath.

"Nope," I said with the same immediacy.

"Why not?" James asked in a tone I recognized. I think I'd used it with my parents when I was twelve and desperately needed a large fry and ice cream from McDonald's.

"Because I want to spend time with the kid I mentor."

Kevin had been struggling with the normal issues of being a fatherless teenager. His mom made me his unofficial godfather a couple of years ago, and since then Kevin has taken to that calling.

"What does that have to do with me?" came the conditioned response.

I thought for a moment. Kevin struggles with homosexuality as well as partying and drugging. It would be an amazing reality for him to confront a forty-five-year-old gay man who is HIV positive and homeless. It might be the wake-up call he needs. I wondered if I could wrap James into a teachable moment. James could share his story with the best of them, and that might be the catalyst for Kevin's life change.

"Okay, you can come," I said with a slightly mischievous tone.

"Great." James smiled victoriously.

Instead of dropping James off, I drove to Christina's apartment. She knew Kevin and his mom well. Her friend Amanda was still in town and was up for it too. James and I walked into the apartment, and I called Kevin.

"Wazzup?" Kevin answered in his usual fashion, pretending not to care about anything.

"You still down for Six Flags today?"

"Yeah, but I'm with my mom at the mall till four."

"Perfect, see you then."

I looked at James, Amanda, and Christina. "We're going at four."

"What time's it now?" James asked.

"Nine."

"What're we gonna do until then?" James looked at Amanda and Christina and then at me in almost desperation.

I started to get irritated but then refrained. "Dude, we'll just chill here, grab some lunch, watch some TV, and then grab Kevin."

The droopy face returned, and I wanted to backhand him.

We turned the TV on and sat on Christina's couch. Christina, Amanda, and I engaged in conversation while James sulked. I felt the life being sucked out of me.

After lunch, my phone rang. It was Kevin.

"Hey, man, I don't think I can make Six Flags tonight."

"What! Come on, man; we had plans."

"Yeah, I know—sorry, but I forgot I made plans with Lexi. But you can come here if you wanna."

Teenagers. I wondered if I was like that when I was sixteen. I'm sure I was, but for a moment I wanted to be self-righteous. I pondered creating a cell-phone shock device that would zap his central nervous system with the touch of a button. But since I was short on time and equipment, I settled for a biting remark.

"Dude, you're killing me. Quit flaking out."

"Sorry, man."

"Okay. We'll be there about eight o'clock tonight. I'm bringing Amanda, Christina, and James."

I turned toward the group. A look of stark terror was on James's face.

"James, we're not going to Six Flags. We're going to Kevin's to hang out with him."

"Why?" James asked.

"Because I mentor him, and part of that is spending time with him. He's a teenager involved in drugs, he's struggling with homosexuality, he's not doing well in school, he's the son of a single parent, and he needs someone to love him."

"What about Six Flags?"

"James, it's not about you." And that was it. James sat back and let his loss settle on his chest.

"Is that cool with you ladies?" They both smiled, trying to calm the tension in the air created by the current discussion.

A couple of movies later we got in Christina's Explorer and ventured to Kevin's place. We decided to take Kevin and his friends to CiCi's. This was quite an escapade, overeating on pizza, laughing at teenagers, and hoping we wouldn't get kicked out. I wanted to steer the conversation toward spiritual things, but I kept getting veered off course by the teenagers' talk of all the drugs and alcohol they had done the previous weekend.

James's demeanor had changed, and he was engaged with everyone and having a generally good time. I relaxed a bit.

We made it back to Kevin's mom's apartment. She was out with her boyfriend, which allowed us to hold a forum on anything from drugs to Jesus. I was looking forward to getting off the drugs and getting on to Jesus. Wading through the latest drug talk was arduous but necessary. Finally, with a small crowd of kids gathered around, I asked James to tell his story.

James talked of his abuse as a child. He spoke of his heartache of growing up and being gay, of being on drugs, and of being homeless. James explained that some people were homeless because they chose that route. They just wanted to do drugs and didn't want to pay any bills, and that lifestyle can only go so far until an eviction notice is posted to your door.

The teenagers were spellbound as he talked about contracting HIV. When James spoke of how God put him in the belly of a whale at the Superdome, Kevin's interest piqued even further. The fact that James was coming through in such a huge way took away any doubts I might have had about him. I was euphoric watching him connect with these teenagers like he was—especially Kevin.

Kevin asked questions as if they were the only two in the room. It was perfect. James even knew how to steer the conversation in a way that when he talked about himself, Kevin felt he was talking about him. I was so proud of James. He really bared his soul.

"Hey, Kevin, I hate to cut you guys off, but it is close to one o'clock in the morning. I'll have to holla' atcha later." (I prided myself on being able to speak "teen.")

We said our goodbyes to the group and started for the door, leaving Kevin pondering as his whole world spun for a moment.

James and I left the women at Christina's apartment and cruised down to my place. A giddy feeling jumped in my gut as I felt like we'd accomplished something.

My phone rang. It was Kevin. He wanted to talk to James. I left the phone with James and went to my room as he talked to Kevin through the night. I prayed for two things: (1) that James would be inspired by the opportunity to influence a young man's life toward Christ and (2) that James's story could influence a kid who needed to hear from the Lord and wake up to the reality that there was a God who loved him and that no relationship or drug could satisfy a void that only God can fill.

Do not follow the crowd in doing wrong. When you give testimony in a lawsuit, do not pervert justice by siding with the crowd, and do not show favoritism to a poor man in his lawsuit.

—from the Book of Exodus

CHAPTER 23: TEARS

It was Scott-Michael's birthday, and the men from SPF7 all headed to a Mediterranean restaurant to celebrate. Bill, Brit, James, and all the guys plus Christina and some of her girlfriends showed up as well to celebrate with Scott-Michael and his family. I could only stay for forty minutes as I had promised one of my high school buddies I would come by and say "hi" at his birthday party, thirty minutes away in Arlington.

I had told James that tonight he'd have to hang with one of the other guys for the evening. I asked Bill if he could take James to his place. James wasn't altogether thrilled with that proposition because he suspected Bill didn't like him very much. He wasn't too far off. However, when Bill agreed, he had no choice but to go with him.

After a rather enthusiastic rendition of *Happy Birthday to You*, we watched Scott-Michael blow out his birthday candles. Ready for the next celebration, I gave the obligatory handshake-backslap to all.

"Hey, Bill, take care of James and go easy on him," I chided as I headed for the door

"You know I will."

I took off toward birthday party number two at the Big Apple Café in Arlington. I said my hellos and goodbyes and then headed home, actually looking forward to a night without James at my apartment. I wandered up my staircase and sat down in my empty kitchen. I looked in my fridge for some munchies and tried to do homework. My mind drifted for a moment to how James was faring with Bill. I imagined Bill's accusing demeanor, making James feel very uncomfortable—but only for a moment. I had Greek to do.

My phone vibrated.

"Hey, guy, I dropped James off down in the 'hood. Kind of a suspicious place. Not sure why he would ever go down there. He had me stop under a light and told me to let him walk up to a certain unlit house. That made me suspicious." As usual, Bill was to the point.

"Why did he want to go down there?"

Bill paused. "He said he had some laundry to do or something."

Sounded familiar. "Okay, man. That's what he tells me."

"Chris, I'm convinced this guy is totally using you. How much money have you given him lately?"

"I don't know. I'm not exactly keeping close tabs on it. I usually give him whatever is in my wallet."

"I'm telling you, Chris, something ain't right down there. There's no reason James should ever go down there to do laundry. It's an excuse to get high."

"Bill, you don't know that."

"****, I don't."

"I'll see you tomorrow, Bill. I'm exhausted. I'm going to sleep."

"I know you always believe the best in people. And I'm glad you do. I'm just here to protect you from doing something stupid and risking your life without reason."

"Thanks, Bill. Good night."

The next morning came, and the light beaming in across the room woke me up before my alarm. I rolled out of bed and climbed to the floor. I glanced into James's room from sheer habit, expecting to see his heavy frame slumped on the ground. For a moment I forgot that he hadn't stayed here last night. Then memory returned, and I continued on with my morning.

Leaving the bathroom with a fresh shave, fresh breath, and a clean body, I got dressed. My cell vibrated.

I grabbed the phone and checked the caller ID. It was a Dallas number, but not one that I knew. Experience taught me that this would be James.

"This is Chris," I answered.

"This is James," came a weak voice. "I'm at the hospital."

"Are you okay?" I could hear sobbing.

"Chris, I'm scared. It's never been like this. I'm scared." For a moment I looked out the window blankly and didn't speak. I didn't know what to say.

"Hello?" James asked filling the silence.

"Are you okay?" I blurted again.

"I don't know. I don't know. I'm at the hospital."

"Okay, okay," I said, gaining back my pastor composure. "Let me pray for you real quick."

I prayed for James and asked God to transform his pain into healing. His tears covered some of my words, but I knew God heard. I wasn't sure what to do. *Should I go to the hospital? But what would I do there? What could I do? Argh. This was painful.*

"I'll call you when I'm done. It may be awhile." I was saved by James.

"Okay, man, I'm praying for you." I felt like I could and should do more, but I didn't. Was it my responsibility?

We hung up, and I sat down at my dining room table for a moment. I glanced at the assortment of papers, envelopes, and textbooks littering the desk. My mind felt like that. What was I supposed to do?

I grabbed my phone and called Bill. "James called me from the hospital, and he sounds real bad. What do you think?" I asked. I knew Bill was suspicious, but I hoped that he might have some deeper insight than a simple "he's guilty."

"I don't know, but I think that it's more than a coincidence that whenever he gets dropped in the 'hood, he ends up at the hospital."

"What are you saying?" I asked.

"I'm just saying I don't know what his deal is . . . and there was fifty bucks missing last night from the dinner. I know you weren't there when that happened, but how would fifty bucks come up missing if he didn't take it?"

"You don't know that, Bill. Someone could have miscounted."

"Maybe, but there's too much stuff that ain't comin' up legit. He knows what he's doing, and I'm just trying to warn you." He paused. "You coming to church?"

"Yeah, I guess," I said.

I hung up the phone and called Brit. He was dumbfounded as well.

"Brit, Bill thinks I'm crazy here. Things with James have been going real well, and now he's in the hospital again."

"Have you ever seen any of his health records or anything?"

"Yeah, he's got a bunch of medical-looking papers in his stuff at my house," I said.

"Maybe we need to not judge him. That's the thing I hate about the church. Judging people based on appearances as opposed to facts. I won't do that, and neither should you. Every time I've taken James to lunch he has broadened my perspective and shown me things in myself that I need to change. See this through," Brit counseled.

"That's what I think. I would rather err on the side of grace."

"Good call. Hey, I've gotta go," Brit said, and we hung up.

Dear God, please get me to the bottom of what is going on with this man.

A generous man will prosper;
he who refreshes others will himself be refreshed.

—from the Book of Proverbs

CHAPTER 24: Flopping

The next morning I awoke to the sound of my alarm clock bellowing at me from the living room. I had to be at Greek study group at seven thirty, where we went over all the homework from the previous class to prepare for today's.

The whole alarm-clock-in-the-other-room thing seemed an infallible way to make sure I didn't sleep in, that I would get showered and be out the door and off to Greek class on time. However, I defeated the alarm by hitting the almighty snooze button. I went back to my room, climbed the ladder, and fell asleep. So much for that.

I awoke nine minutes later and began the hurried process of getting myself ready to learn Greek. Without James, I had more time to get to school since a side trip to the DRC sometimes took thirty extra minutes.

With James at the hospital, I knew he'd eventually call, giving *me*, the hero of our story, yet another opportunity to minister and be the light of Christ to him.

Can I be honest here? I dreaded it. I didn't want to be the light of Christ to someone that day. There was a part of me that really wished he would never call again. I was tired. This nagging feeling, like I deserved something more out of James, kept creeping into my soul. I wondered how Jesus did it. The guy was always surrounded by people with needs. He always had to be the guy responsible for reaching out to the down-and-out. I chose to follow Jesus, and now I was starting to see what he meant by pick up your cross and die daily.[1]

Okay, Lord, I'm dying here.

I went to Greek class and tried to pay attention. My mind wandered in and out of Dr. Hoe's communication about the Word of God in a dead language. After class, as I walked to my car, my cell phone rang. The unknown number told me it was the hospital, and soon I would be on my way to pick up James. I dreaded it. I just needed a break.

"This is James. You can come and pick me up, man." He sounded cheerful.

"Hey, I've got some things I need to take care of. I'm going call Brit real quick and see if he can come and get you."

I called Brit. "Hey, do you mind grabbin' James from the hospital? I think I'm needing a break from him today."

"Bro, I'm working on a new board in the garage." He paused. "Can someone else do it?"

"Yeah, I guess so," I said, defeated.

"Wait, man. I'll go and get him. Which hospital?" The defeat in my voice must have manipulated—er—influenced him to change his mind. And at this point, I didn't care.

"I usually grab him from Baylor's emergency room."

"I'll pick him up and then bring him to SPF7 tonight."

"Sweet, man. Thanks."

I sighed and let the weight of James shift off my shoulders for a moment.

I felt like I was at Ranger School in the army. Amid learning the best ways to endure the elements, we also went on these long walks called patrols, carrying sixty- to eighty-pound rucksacks. Whenever we would pause to check our compass to see if we were headed in the right direction or to do a head count to make sure we hadn't lost anyone, a few of us would break all military bearing and flop on our backs for a moment. We weren't quitting, and if we saw any instructors around, we would never do it, but every now and then, we just flopped.

Once in the Florida phase I decided to carry a lot of ammo to make up for the fact that I had been falling asleep in the patrol base. I wanted to make up for that and really be a team player. We also did peer grading, and I was feeling a little behind, and I figured carrying the ammo for the men might put me in a better light with the guys. However, my body, weakened by two months of food and sleep deprivation, couldn't muster it. Looking back, I realize it had to have weighed an unexaggerated eighty-five to ninety pounds.

After walking hours through the night on very few calories, I staggered on the patrol. I was fighting to keep up with the pace of the march. I fought back the tears as my shoulder muscles burned. I kept adjusting the weight of the rucksack from the bone to the shoulder muscle, hoping to alleviate the pain. However, the fire continued to burn hotter in my muscles and tendons, and the only voice I could hear in my head was my inner screaming monologue, *Stop! Just quit! Stop!*

I couldn't pray while walking because that took the concentration off moving. Periodically we came to short halts. That was a five-minute stop for the patrol leaders to do a map check and make sure they knew where they were. Every time we stopped, I prayed with everything I had for God to give me strength. Anger actually dipped into my prayer. Finally, at wits' end, I asked another Ranger buddy for help. He looked at me like I was a little girl for a moment. But when I opened my ruck and let him peer inside, he found me carrying almost thirty-five pounds of ammo alone.

He looked at me and asked, "What the **** you carrying all this for?"

"I don't know." I grimaced.

"Here gimme some of this. I'll spread the rest out." He took that ammunition and distributed it across the squad. I thanked God for that Ranger student. I don't remember his name, but I remember that night.

Right now, I was flopping. Right now I needed someone to come and pick up the weight. Brit came through as he had more and more on this journey, and I was thankful that somebody could. I didn't feel spiritual, and I didn't feel full of hope. I just felt tired. I get that way, every now and then when I get low. I couldn't even blame James really. It's just that my shoulders were burning, and I needed someone else to bear the burden for a while. *That's not too much to ask, is it?*

And the things you have heard me say in the presence of many witnesses entrust to reliable men who will also be qualified to teach others.

—from the Second Letter to Timothy

CHAPTER 25: LARRY

A couple of hours later I was headed back to the seminary to get ready for SPF7. My four-hour sabbatical from James had done me good.

My cell phone vibrated. I struggled, doing what felt like a weird yoga position while driving sixty-five miles an hour in traffic as I pulled out my phone, leaving my pants pocket hanging over the gearshift.

It was Bill.

"Hey, guy, be there on time tonight. I have a buddy from AA coming for the first time." *Like I'm ever late*, I thought, but I let it go. His straightforward caustic nature at times can cause people to flinch. But his heart is truly as big as the state in which we reside. Bill is the ultimate inviter. In fact, he is the one who organized SPF7 in the beginning.

I arrived fifteen minutes earlier than usual, got my computer set up, and made sure the projector and software were running perfectly.

The men started to pile in. A lot of new faces met the old. Backslaps and handshakes combined with swear words and laughter. I felt a warmth among the group as the rawness of life was expressed. It is a man environment. To be honest, if you've been in church for too long, you might be uncomfortable here. There's not an ounce of pretension.

To get the men to sit down and get started, I asked Bill to lead us in prayer. We then went around the room, introducing the new guys.

"Okay, fellas, introduce yourself by stating your name and your favorite beverage."

"Beer," Brit responded. "I want a lager right now." I smiled. Everyone laughed. This was Dallas Seminary. No drinking allowed. Larry was next.

"I'm an alcoholic," he started. "I can't drink alcohol without falling off the wagon. I'm trying to stay clear of it. I like water."

Brit's face turned red, and he put his head in his hands for a moment.

"I'm glad you're here," I said.

"Me too," the rest of the men proclaimed.

We went around the group, finished introducing ourselves, and then started digging into the Word. We talked about the betrayer, Judas Iscariot, and his role in the Gospel.

After the Bible study, we went to prayer requests.

James spoke up. "Well, for those who don't know, I'm homeless. But what I was wantin' us to pray about is us havin' a feeding for three hundred people at the Day Resource Center on Halloween."

"Why Halloween?" Brit asked.

"I want to commemorate the day I rededicated my life to Christ. It was at a homeless shelter a couple years back on Halloween, and this man came up to me. Black man. Old guy. He kept talkin' about how God was so good and I could trust him. There was somethin' different about that guy. I remember askin' him if he really believed all this stuff about God was true. He just gripped my hand and said, 'I know it's true.' That's all it took for me to just know that there is a God and that he has this whole thing under control."

"So what exactly do you want to do?" Bill asked.

"I just want to get a big feedin' together and give some people some hope. This is what God is showin' me I'm gonna do."

The group gave James a nod.

"Oh, hey, one more thing. Please pray that I get an ID soon. I'm tellin' you I can't get a job without it."

"I can testify to that," I added. It plagued my soul, because I felt the weight of his need.

"Also, I just wanna thank all y'all for all the help. I'm not always the best at sayin' this, but Chris has really stuck his neck out for me. I appreciate it. Brit too, thanks. All y'all really have made an impact on my life, and I just know things are gonna get better."

A tear crested my eyelid as I felt that fuzzy warmth tickle my soul. I knew I was probably losing reward in heaven, but I hoped it would inspire other guys to help.

STUMBLING SOULS

Another one of the guys stated that he had decided to accept the challenge I gave during the Bible study to do something risky for Christ. I smiled and wondered if he would be up for a night with James.

Larry then gave his prayer request. "I really don't know how to pray. I'm a drunk, and like I said to Bill, I've never been around an environment like this. I'm new to the Bible, and I don't like church. I don't like the music at Fellowship, and no one has talked to me yet there. I'm also about to go on a drinking binge. I'm having trouble finding meaning in life. I'm just glad I now have someone to sit with next Sunday."

We prayed, and afterward Michael Riley and another guy in his midthirties pounced on Larry. I couldn't help but overhear their conversation.

"Hey, man, you can call us anytime. We're there for you," Michael Riley said. "SPF7 has changed my life. I never prayed aloud before, and I never thought I was good enough until a month ago." He continued to share about how his life had changed and what it meant to harness the power of Christ.

I listened to these men who had matured and grown in Christ share how he had changed their lives. Emotion stirred in me, causing my eyes to water. My soul shook a bit as I heard phrases I'd said to them repeated to Larry. It's that whole fly-on-the-wall thing, hearing my words come out of their mouths. I can't tell you what that feels like. Then I wondered if that's how Christ feels when I repeat the things he has taught me, and then the guys I've taught repeat them to someone else. That might be what he meant when he said, "*What I say to you in the dark, tell in the light, and what is whispered in your ear, proclaim from the housetops.*"[1] Here these guys were, speaking in that moment many of the things that I had heard from Christ in my time with him, and now they were proclaiming it from rooftops.

Once I finished rearranging the room, I glanced to my left and saw Larry talking to James out in the hallway. James motioned to me to come out there. I moved gingerly, not sure what was about to happen.

James said, "Larry might have a job for me."

Larry spoke candidly, "I'm a Realtor. I have some houses that I'm cleaning up. I need someone to do it for me. If James needs a job, I can hire him for a hundred dollars a day. I need to know if you think that's something he can do and if we can trust him to do it."

"Absolutely," I said without hesitation.

"Great. Can you get him to my office in the morning?"

"No problem." I smiled from ear to ear.

"One more thing, he can stay in the house until we sell it as well. And if this goes well, he can clean the next house and the next house and be making a hundred dollars a day as long as he wants."

My jaw almost hit the floor.

This was it. This is what we had been praying for. If James could do this, he would be free, and we could worry about the ID later. I mean, financial freedom was right around the corner. I did a small victory dance in my head. God had done it. All James had to do was show up and work, and everything would be taken care of!

For if the willingness is there, the gift is acceptable according to what one has, not according to what he does not have. Our desire is not that others might be relieved while you are hard pressed, but that there might be equality.

—from the Second Letter to the Corinthians

CHAPTER 26: WORK

The next morning the alarm woke me up, and excitement pulsed through my arteries and veins in anticipation of taking James to work. This could be the last day that James would ever have to be here. This could also be the day that my prayers from the past couple of months would finally come to fruition. I could now answer the doubters who questioned if God still changed lives and point them to James as a walking testimonial billboard. I showered, got dressed, and woke up James.

"Hey, man, you takin' a shower?"

"Nah, I'm good. If I'm cleanin', I'll just get dirty again anyway."

"But, James . . ." Before I could finish the thought, James's face interjected, informing me that to argue this further would only frustrate me. "Never mind."

No sense in tainting his mood for his first day. A day of work had enough troubles of its own. I hadn't really seen James's work ethic in action, but if it was anything like his daily attitude, it would bounce from energetic to lethargic depending on which way the wind blew through Dallas.

We left my gated driveway as usual, James ducking down in the car while I kept a steady eye out for my landlords. I hoped this would be our final stealth departure.

It just so happened that Larry worked two miles down the street from me. We turned on Greenville Avenue and headed toward Larry's office. I felt a knot in my stomach like when I was sixteen and my dad took me to get my first job at McDonald's. Although nervous on the first day, I soon grew to love my time at Mickey D's. I wanted this to work out for James. In reality he had been through several employments and terminations, so all the tension that I assumed he should be feeling nestled into my neck and shoulders.

We parked the car in the real estate office parking garage. Before getting out, I grabbed James's shoulder and prayed for him, asking God to give him a good attitude and a face that looked like he wanted to be there. I had reminded James before that his face looked like his dog just died every time he met someone new, and generally that wouldn't win him any friends. It was in God's hands now. We got out and walked into the real estate office. I asked the receptionist for Larry, and she pushed an intercom button to let him know I was there. Then she looked at James.

"Can I help you?" she asked uncomfortably.

"He's with me," I quickly answered. I was almost annoyed by her asking that. But I guess we didn't look like we came together as James had a tendency not to stand beside me or look like he was with me. He'd just look at the ground awkwardly when I addressed people. James wasn't exactly dressed for success either. Despite my urging, he hadn't taken a shower. The apartment was starting to smell like feet again.

"Oh." The receptionist felt stupid for a moment, smiled, then acted as if she was about to do something really important.

Larry entered the waiting room. His smile indicated all was still good to go. I followed him back into his office, James in tow. Larry took a quick phone call, which allowed me to admire all the running awards that Larry had won. Larry might be a drunk, but he was a fast drunk. I looked at his marathon times on the wall and shook my head. *Wow.*

Larry hung up and then looked at James and with great enthusiasm asked, "You ready?"

"I guess. Yes. I'm ready," said James in a manner that signified more issues than I wanted to deal with at the moment.

Larry laid it out. "James, I'm going to pay you one hundred dollars a day until the job's done. I have needed somebody for so long for this—so thank you."

James gave a weak smile, and if I'd had a cattle prod, I would have shocked him. I let the moment pass. I figured he could handle himself.

"I'm outta here." I started walking toward the door. "Let me know if you need anything, Larry. Also, please let me know when James needs to be picked up or what the deal is, and I'll come and get him."

James was about to be on his own in a good way. I felt nervous for James and for Larry. Larry was risking a lot for a guy who'd only been to our Bible study once. I wondered what God was up to.

I'll be honest. I left the office with a newfound freedom, but I also had a weird feeling about leaving James there. I thought that he might go into the doldrums. I gave Larry a call a couple of hours later.

"Larry, how's it going?"

"It's going great. I bought all the supplies for James and am excited to see how he's going to work out."

"How's his attitude?"

"Great. He looks like he'll be a hard worker, and this could turn into a nice small business for him, if that's what he really wants."

"Awesome, Larry. Thanks for doing this," I said.

"No, I needed him. This is a perfect fit."

"God is awesome."

"Yes, he is," said Larry. "Hey, are you going to be in church on Sunday?"

"I'll be there. See you then."

I hung up the phone, and electricity surged through me. James was really working. He was really going to be able to do this. I was leaving for Cleveland tomorrow, and James now had a place to stay out of the 'hood. *God, you are good.*

The prayer of a righteous man is powerful and effective. Elijah was a man just like us. He prayed earnestly that it would not rain, and it did not rain on the land for three and a half years. Again he prayed, and the heavens gave rain, and the earth produced its crops.[1]

God had heard my prayer. He had stopped the famine and was bringing the rain. Now this is the kind of rain I don't mind.

"What do you think? There was a man who had two sons. He went to the first and said, 'Son, go and work today in the vineyard.' 'I will not,' he answered, but later he changed his mind and went. Then the father went to the other son and said the same thing. He answered, 'I will, sir,' but he did not go. Which of the two did what his father wanted?" "The first," they answered.

—from the Gospel of Matthew

CHAPTER 27: CLEVELAND

With James in Larry's hands, I left for Cleveland. It's a steel city that looks exactly how I felt—tired. After I made a connection in Chicago, my flight arrived in Cleveland, and I made it to my hotel around seven. I threw my stuff on the bed and went to the prison ministry guest-speaker meeting.

I'm a part of an international prison ministry called Bill Glass Champions for Life. They hold events in prisons around the world, sharing hope with people who really could use it. My role in the ministry is to share army stories that can somehow be related to God and his love for people.

At the meeting, we were told where we'd be speaking and whom we'd be partnered with the following day in the prisons. I surveyed the mixed bag of Christians who were everything from Super Bowl champions to Ultimate Fighters to ex-cons. I loved these weekends as they again gave me a chance to see light shine into the darkness.

I was told I'd be partnered with Brenda Harp, a singer and songwriter based out of California. I was excited to tell her about the incredible stuff going on with James, but that would have to wait until tomorrow. I went back to my room at the Ramada Inn and barely got my shoes off before falling asleep.

I awoke the next morning still exhausted from my travels and the stress of studying Greek. I hoped that the dank air of my hotel room would soon be replaced by something better outside. However, we were in downtown Cleveland. I smiled as I noticed the cigarette burn in my comforter. *Hey, prison ministry ain't supposed to be luxurious.* I went over to the sink, half expecting brown water to drip from it, and smiled when it looked and tasted clean. I brushed my teeth and shaved.

My cell phone buzzed. Larry's name on my caller ID instantly filled me with dread. *Why would Larry be calling this early on a Friday morning?*

"Chris, this is Larry." His voice had that intonation of stress that I was accustomed to in people who were overworked and feeling burdened by life.

"Hey! What's up, man?" I said with my usual almost overly happy tone. It was all I could do not to be a smart aleck and say, "Yeah, I know."

"It's James, man. He didn't show up today, and I'm stuck."

"I'm so sorry." I felt responsible. I had vouched for James. "Look, let me call some people and see what I can find out. I'm sorry for putting you in a bind."

"It's no problem. I just hope he's all right and nothing bad happened to him," Larry said flatly.

I did too.

We hung up, and I sat down and tried to wrap my head around the situation. I really didn't know what James would or could do. Things have been going well, really well. And now he doesn't show up? From Cleveland, I could do nothing. I felt horrible, because I was the one who gave Larry the okay on James. Maybe James was in the hospital again.

I called Bill.

"James didn't show up to work for Larry today. I think I left him hanging. Or maybe something happened to James. I thought James would be staying in the house he was cleaning, but he's not there."

"Chris, I told you this would get you in trouble. Look, guy, he's still on drugs."

"We don't know that."

"Chris, when I dropped James off in the 'hood the other week, he wouldn't let me drive him up to the door. He made me park down by the light, and then he walked up to the house. In the world of drugs and crime they do that because they have lookouts. If James were to drive right up to a crack house in that neighborhood with a white guy, they wouldn't let him in because they would think he was with a cop. That's the way these operations work."

I didn't want to believe that. "Maybe he got sick and went to the hospital."

"That's another thing. Every time he misses something important, he's in the hospital. I wonder if that's a coincidence."

"Bill, it could be," I said.

"Look, Chris, during my twenty years as a police officer, I have learned that those who've had a traumatic event in their lives tend to be quiet about it. The two main reasons people talk about it, in my opinion, are this: they're either talking about the tragedy to help others through a similar event, sharing their story and how they got through it. Or they have their hand out and are looking for sympathy and capitalizing off of it."

"I don't know, Bill," I said frustrated. "I'm here in Cleveland about to go into the prisons and can't do a single thing from here. Can you call Larry and make sure he's okay?"

I didn't want to think about it anymore. It was not the time to let James intrude upon my opportunity to share the gospel here, but I couldn't let go of it.

"No problem."

Bill hung up, and I found my eyes inspecting the dirty carpet. I was tired of having to deal with this drama. I was tired of feeling like there were secrets behind everything. Bill was convinced that James wasn't only on drugs, but manipulating me and everyone else for his own purposes. Maybe Bill was overly suspicious? Wasn't that how most people viewed homeless people? With suspicion? Had Bill's cop life interfered with his ability to see the best in people and perhaps marred the fact that we have an overcoming Savior? Although prayers were being answered, James's heart hadn't seemed to change. Maybe Bill really did see reality, and I had been blinded by my pair of rose-colored glasses.

This is messy. Life is messy. Faith is messy. *Lord, talk to me here. What's going on?* The Holy Spirit hadn't impressed anything in my heart other than to serve James by following the book of James. From Cleveland I could do nothing but pray. I got down on the dirty carpet and placed my head on the cigarette-burned comforter and prayed for the Lord to hear me and give me wisdom and to be with James. After praying, I got up and finished dressing.

This is disconcerting. When you take someone home to live with you to get him on his feet, he's supposed to get on his feet. Especially when the sole reason you do it is out of obedience to God. And now my obedience in trying to get James on his feet was perhaps causing others to stumble. *Would this cause Larry to relapse?*

I paused for a moment to let God regain his rule over the world. All I could do was love James. How James's life ended would be up to God and James. With that thought firmly fastened in my mind, I headed out of my room and down to the lobby to catch my ride to enter the prisons of Cleveland.

All hard work brings a profit,
but mere talk leads only to poverty.

—from the Book of Proverbs

CHAPTER 28: QUESTION

I lay in bed Saturday morning at the Ramada Inn, recovering from a night of battling the stale air and an overly loud air conditioner for much-needed rest. Friday had been incredible. I was introduced as a semi rock star to a prison yard full of hard men. My military experience of dealing with death in battle gave me credibility with these men who had similar experiences on the streets of Cleveland. The Bill Glass Champions for Life Prison Ministry harvested every story I could recall to draw men to Christ.

I had preached twice and spent the day getting to know some prisoners who asked me all sorts of questions from whether a felon could get into the army to how many people I had killed. Others shared with me their heartfelt stories. One man informed me that he was a child molester. His fellow inmates despised him. In their eyes, he was beneath them. He told me how one day a bunch of men had gathered together to beat him. He believed they intended to kill him. A Christian prisoner stood between them and wouldn't allow it. He never forgot that and, as a result, dedicated his life to Christ.

He looked at me with wide round eyes and simply asked, "But what about the shame?"

I stared back at him, looking for the words.

"Does it ever go away?" he asked.

"Yeah, yeah, it goes away," I said.

I told him about the fact that God does not hold our sins against us. "Do you know the story of John 8 and the woman caught in adultery?"

"Yeah, I heard it."

"Man, there is an awesome verse I want you to hold on to whenever you ask that question." I repeated verse 11 to him: "Neither do I condemn you."

He just looked at me.

"Hey, man, you're not condemned. Check it out; even after the conversation with Jesus, the next day that woman still had to face people saying all sorts of condemning stuff to her. The women at the market, the people in the streets—who had all seen her in her birthday suit and a sheet—the men calling her less-than-lovely names; they didn't just all of a sudden forget. Jesus didn't do the Jedi mind trick on Jerusalem and make them forget her naked appearance in the temple. All that woman had to go on for her forgiveness were Jesus' words 'Neither do I condemn you.'"

"Yeah, that's cool." His eyes watered.

"Because you're forgiven, you are now able to go and leave your life of sin. What goes on the cross stays on the cross."

That man looked at me and then studied his shoes.

"Will you pray for me?"

"Yeah, man, I can do that."

I prayed for him and watched his face wrinkle as I felt God's grace envelop him. He still had a tough road ahead, as he had to face constant condemnation here in the prison as well as on the outside. That man is forgiven in the eyes of God, although the consequences of his sin will still affect him. *But for the grace of God, there go I.*

I left the prison, reveling in what God could do. There is something about hanging out with prisoners and seeing the Light befall men's faces that encourages my heart. It empowers me to continue to minister to the "least of these." Studying Greek grammar in meticulous detail with no reward often leaves me wondering why I do it. But facing a man who needs grace reminds me that my studying has deep purpose. I get to convey grace to people who are desperate to know it. Very few feelings can compare to it.

The next morning, I got out of bed and moved to the sink for the routine teeth brushing. I was grateful that I didn't have to be in the prison until noon. I stood there, staring in the mirror, wondering what had become of James, and pondering if he had experienced shame like the prisoner I visited with yesterday. I was also thinking of eating breakfast at Bob Evans and getting out of this hotel room. My cell phone vibrated, rudely interrupting my thoughts of pancakes and an omelet.

"This is Chris," I answered, hoping that it was James calling to tell me he got everything worked out.

"This is James." His voice was high pitched and stressed. "I'm at the house that Larry told me to go to, and Larry hasn't paid me yet, so I don't know what's going on."

"James, did you show up yesterday?" I asked carefully.

"No, I was in the hospital, okay? I was in the hospital!" I could feel James's grip tighten on his own phone.

"Did you call Larry?"

"Yes, but he's not answering. I've cleaned this place, and I just need him to come down and make sure that he pays me." For a moment, I felt like the whole world was on my shoulders.

"James, I'm in Cleveland. If you called Larry, and he didn't answer, I don't know what to tell you. Here, do this. Call Bill."

"You want me to call Bill?" he asked, tension in his voice causing his vocal chords to strain.

"Yes, I do, James. I'll talk to you later."

"Okay, man, bye."

Above all, my brothers, do not swear—not by heaven or by earth or by anything else. Let your "Yes" be yes, and your "No," no, or you will be condemned.

—from the Letter of James

CHAPTER 29: CONFRONTATION

I got back to Dallas from Cleveland on Saturday night, and as I made my way to church on Sunday, I couldn't help but feel a little wonder and a little dread about what would happen next. My phone vibrated.

"This is Chris."

"Hey, guy, you on your way?" It was Bill. "I called the hospitals yesterday, both Baylor and Parkland, and neither of them have a record of James staying there on Friday. So he's lying." Bill almost sounded cheerful.

"Okay," I said without emotion.

"Look, you need to talk to him. He needs to be confronted. I can't do it because, well, he already knows that I have him found out. We've got to keep him from Larry because who knows if Larry will just go off and start drinking. He is a nonconfrontational type of guy. Larry said that James was very disrespectful and almost belligerent on the phone with him. So we got to make sure we don't have a scene at church."

"Okay, I got it," I said, not wanting to be a leader today. I knew, however, that this was the price to be paid for being the guy who took James into my apartment and the guy who challenges people to put Christ first and live a life of being second.

I wondered if I had been bold or stupid. It was my problem, especially if he was getting out of control. To be honest, I felt sorry for myself, but this was what made life exciting. I like being the guy who makes hard decisions and has to be the bearer of justice and mercy. Yet, that doesn't mean it's painless.

I arrived at church and said hi to the usual groups of people. I was running a little late, so I went in and found a seat off to the side, not my normal front-and-center place. After the service, I went out to find Bill. Out of the corner of my eye, I caught James sitting on one of the couches in the lobby. *Great, here we go.*

Bill motioned to me, and I walked over to him.

"Chris, he's sitting on the couches. I'll try and find Larry and make sure they don't run into each other. Tell him the deal, and let's get out of here."

I didn't know what I was going to say. I still felt I didn't have all the information. I knew Bill was convinced that James was a liar and that nothing he said could be true. I wasn't so sure. I started walking over to him and observed his face. It was droopy, but he looked a little more confident. His clothes looked like they needed washing, but he was shaven. I sat down next to him on the couch.

"What's up, James?" I asked, trying to be as cool as the other side of a pillow.

"What's up?" James replied without emotion or even a glance in my direction. He stared off toward the ceiling. I suspected he was counting ceiling tiles.

I decided to get right to the point. "What happened, James? Shoot me straight. Why didn't you show up to work?"

He let a few people pass by, making their way to lunch with friends, while others stuck around to mingle and talk.

"I told you. I was at the hospital."

"James, Bill called the hospital. They have no record of a James Rudolph being there. What's going on? Are you lying?" I asked with sincerity and tried not to provoke him. The reaction James gave wasn't what I was hoping for but rather what I was expecting. He gave me the look that a child gives when he's caught in the act of misbehaving but is acting obnoxiously innocent.

"The hospital loses records all the time," James replied, his voice barely tempered. He caught himself and calmed down as he watched the crowds pass by. "Look, I was there. They sometimes don't keep records like that."

I wanted to believe him, but I didn't. However, I wondered if the Holy Spirit would convict him. I wanted to believe the best in people. I knew how it felt to tell the truth and have no one believe you. I started to wonder if I was becoming a bleeding-heart liberal.

"Are you okay, James?" I asked with genuine concern.

"Yeah, I'm fine now."

"What was the problem?"

"Same as before. Mild heart attack."

"I see. Why didn't you call Larry?"

"I didn't think about it."

"Did you know that Larry was depending on you to get the job done and that he had to call an owner and give an answer as to why the house had no one working on it? Do you think that made Larry want to drink?"

"That's not fair. I'm not responsible for Larry's drinking."

"Fair enough," I said. "Look, you cannot demand payment when you did not show up. You didn't uphold your end of the deal. You should have cleaned and finished the houses, but you need to tell Larry that you're sorry and that he doesn't owe you anything."

"But I did the work."

"Dude, you didn't show up. He went out on a limb for you."

James sighed.

"Look, James, tomorrow show up at the Bible study, apologize to Larry, and everything can go back to normal."

"So, you want me just to say, 'I'm sorry.'" The look on his face showed signs of sarcasm.

"No, I want you to mean 'I'm sorry.'" I was tired of the game. I felt like James was trying to play me like a shady politician. I wondered if this was how it was with everyone he encountered or if my frustration in the moment was causing me to vilify the innocent.

"Look, if you show up tomorrow at the Bible study and you apologize, that shows me you care. It will all go back to normal." I started to wonder if I wanted things to go back to normal or if they could ever go back to normal. But I had said it, and unless he didn't follow through, I had to do my part.

I put my hand on James's shoulder and prayed. I sensed that James wasn't engaged in the prayer so I glanced at him for a moment, long enough to see his eyes fixated on nothing in particular. I continued praying, asking God to open his heart to him. Although I knew God heard, it felt like James's attitude was firmly impeding my prayer's progress.

I got up, and we both left the building.

He who conceals his sins does not prosper,
but whoever confesses and renounces them finds mercy.

—from the Book of Proverbs

CHAPTER 30: INTERVENTION

"Chris, I need you to listen to this."

The official start time for our Bible study was still several minutes away, and it wasn't like Bill to be early. He took out a mini-recorder. I rolled my eyes as he hit play. It was a conversation between him and another guy.

I heard Bill's gruff voice: "Did you fire James because he didn't have an ID?"

Another voice responded, "No, no, man. I never fired him. We had a whole package deal set up for him. He just quit showing up."

"He just quit showin' up?" Bill's voice queried. "How long had he worked at Landry's?"

"About a week or so, I guess."

"And he just quit showin' up?" Bill asked again.

"Yeah."

Bill shut off the recorder. He made no attempt to hide his Cheshire cat smile. I slumped in my chair and looked up at the ceiling.

"Crud. I guess that proves it."

"I tried to tell you, Chris. He's on drugs. You've given him so much money, and he has blown it all on drugs. You're a good kid. You're just a little naive."

"Yeah, maybe you're right. I still want to give him a chance to come clean. I mean, I told him if he would apologize to Larry everything would go back to normal. I've got to give him that chance. If he admits the truth, then I'm going have him come back to my place."

"Whatever, man. It's your call, but he's gonna lie. That's what he is—a liar."

I really wanted Bill to be wrong.

Soon others started showing up. Brit brought James, and we had a quorum. I wanted to wait to see if Larry would show, but he didn't. *Oh well.* I figured that for James, apologizing to the group could count as an apology to Larry.

"Hey, men, before we start, James has something he wants to say to everyone."

James looked down, and for a moment I wasn't sure if he would actually say anything. Slowly, he pushed his chair back away from the table and stood up.

"Guys, I just wanted to let you know that I let everyone here down. I didn't show up to work on Saturday after Larry had gotten me a job. I was in the hospital, but I probably could've called. I know that all of you are going out on a limb for me. So, I apologize to all y'all."

"Thanks, James." As I spoke those words, I wondered if he really meant anything he had said or if he merely gave in to me telling him he had to say it.

I got everyone focused once again on Matthew 11, and we dove into the character of these men who would take the message of Christ to the world. As we talked, Larry quietly slipped in. Everything in me wanted to stop and have James apologize again right then and there, but it would have been awkward. I figured I'd wait until the end of the night.

We took prayer requests, but no one was ready to share about personal issues. The barometric pressure rose significantly when Larry walked in. It felt like only a matter of time before the room would explode. Finally, we prayed and asked God to protect, be with, and all the normal Christian jargon that goes along with people praying.

"Amen."

"I need everyone to leave except James, Larry, Brit, and Bill," I commanded as the study ended. I didn't mean to come off so tough guy, but this was a tough situation. I had dealt with circumstances like this before in the army, and I think the commander in me took over.

Everyone started to scatter like billiard balls on a hard break as they saw my usual smile turn to granite.

The air conditioner hummed. From my spot at the head of the table, I couldn't help but shake my head at this ragtag group. Could these guys possibly resemble what Christ had in mind when he said to go and make disciples? To my right, Larry gazed at the ceiling. Bill sat to my left, staring laser beams into James's skull. He was as giddy as . . . a tough, crusty cop waiting to destroy a criminal. Beside him, Brit's eyes were downcast, his expression unreadable. I wondered what he was thinking as he stared at his empty hands. He and his wife had invited James over for dinner earlier that night, and he'd really gotten to know James over the past couple of months—or had he? Had anyone? James shifted his gaze, looking past me to my right at the pictures on the wall. I searched his face for any sign of honesty.

"James, I know you apologized to the group earlier about what happened with Larry. But I want you to apologize to him here, now, in person."

We all looked at James. I let the silence rest on him.

"Okay," James said with zero emotion. "Larry, I want to apologize to you for letting you down. I told the group earlier I was sorry. You don't owe me anything. I'm sorry for what I did."

Larry was clearly surprised. "Wow, James, thanks so much. I wasn't expecting that, but I really appreciate it."

"Thanks, Larry," I said. "Would you please excuse us now?"

Larry rose silently and headed for the door.

"James, I know I told you that if you came and apologized, everything would go back to the way it was. But I have a problem. I won't beat around the bush here. There is an issue with your ID. Why did you lose your job at Landry's?"

"I didn't have an ID."

"James, are you sure? Please don't lie to me."

He looked confused. "What do you want me to say? I didn't have an ID, so they fired me." His tone was deliberate.

"James, I heard the manager say that you stopped showing up and that you were never fired." I said this so matter-of-factly that James looked directly at me, wide eyed. The whites of his eyes were tinged red by a network of spindly veins—nothing unusual.

"What do you want me to say?" he asked, throwing his hands in the air.

"The truth, James. The truth," said Brit as he raised his head and looked at James for a moment. "We just want you to tell us the truth. What's going on?"

Bill could contain himself no longer. "James, how long have you been on crack?" he blurted. Bill has only one tool in his problem-solving toolbox—a hammer. Every problem he sees is a nail. In James, he had found the perfect project.

My eyes grew wide. This had not been part of the plan. Bill jumped straight from lying to doing drugs. He was a little out of line, but I knew that this was probably a police technique he had learned from years on the force. I had done the same thing in Iraq with terrorists, but this guy was our friend. To think he might be on drugs was one thing, but to accuse him flat out like this was another.

"You think I'm on drugs?" James asked, clinging to his last shred of dignity.

"I know you are," Bill replied. "I'm an alcoholic. I have been where you are. I know the signs. You had us drop you off at a crack house in the 'hood, and you didn't want the lookouts to see us."

James looked down.

Bill was on a roll. "You've been lying to us. After all the help we've given you. You're on drugs!" He pounded the table to drive the point home.

"Bill, that's enough!" I had to step in. Bill was completely wound up on adrenaline. The muscles tightened around his flushed face, and his neck and shoulders stiffened.

I decided to cool things down. "Listen, James, we love you. I wouldn't have asked you to live with me if I didn't trust and love you. But something has got to change. There are some things that don't add up. And we're here to help you. But we can't do that if you don't level with us."

Brit measured his words carefully. He was the perfect yin to Bill's yang. "Look, James, just man up. Just man up. All you have to do is take responsibility. Larry came in here on his first week and shared his whole heart. He told us straight up that he was a drunk and that he needed help. He was vulnerable. There were no secrets. Did we judge him?"

Silence.

"Did we?" Brit's gaze was gentle but unyielding.

"No."

"Of course not. It's the same thing here." Brit looked at his hands.

"You're on drugs!" Bill exclaimed. "I know you are!" With his distinctive southern accent and handlebar mustache, I saw the fleeting image of Yosemite Sam. I imagined Bill hopping mad, shooting holes in the ceiling with a gigantic pair of pistols. I thought he'd lost his mind, and, to tell the truth, I was about to lose all respect that I had ever held for him. Then I noticed a drastic change in James's demeanor.

"Of *course*, I'm on drugs. You guys have known that all along," James said, as if he were on trial and was making the great confession.

My jaw dropped. Bill had been right all along. I opened my mouth to talk, but words wouldn't come.

Brit broke the silence. "Actually, we didn't know that, James."

"Do you think I would look like this if I weren't on drugs? I mean, look at me! Look at how much money y'all have given me . . . and I still look like this."

I recalled all those nights James had spent "doing laundry." I glanced down at his shirt, stained and reeking of body odor. I remembered the smelly-sock stench that had permeated my apartment. *Man, had I missed it.* I guess I was naive. It had crossed my mind before that perhaps James was on drugs. But I couldn't let myself believe it. When he said all the right things about holiness, when he spoke the Christian lingo, I had taken his word for it. I wanted to believe that Christ's power had changed James's life. Maybe I didn't want to let go of the dream that I, *with a capital "Me,"* had been the one to make a difference. Yet, there he was dejected, the dilapidated fence that every kid in the neighborhood walks by and kicks. My heart sank.

"What are you afraid of, James?" Bill asked. If a hammer was Bill's only tool, the "fear angle" was his only emotional insight.

Silence.

"What are you afraid of?" Bill again hammered the question, and James retreated into an invisible hole.

"I'm going to get an answer! What are you afraid of?" Bill's eyes were bulging. I thought this tactic was overly dramatic, but I had already been proved way wrong, so I said nothing. I stood up and drew closer to James.

"You don't understand what it's like out there," James said with soft resolution. "You don't know where I've been."

"********!" Bill exclaimed. "I've seen more **** than you could ever fathom. Don't tell me I don't know what it's like. Stop being a victim. You had it easy. Chris *gave* you a place to stay. Brit's been *giving* you money. Larry *gave* you a job. All you had to do was behave, suit up, and show up, and you woulda had it made. But you chose to throw it away!"

James muttered something unintelligible.

"James," I started and then paused, wondering if he could hear us anymore. "James, do you want help?"

"I don't know," he answered.

There it was. His hope had died somewhere along the way, and he didn't want help—not tonight, anyway.

"Thanks for your honesty," Brit said, looking into James's droopy face.

"James, I would be willing to pay for your rehab. I would do anything to help you. Whatever it costs, I would pay it, because I love you." I was surprised by the pleading in my own voice.

"****, you can get it for free," Bill said.

"James, do you want help?" I asked.

Silence.

"James, I want you to think about this. You aren't staying with me tonight. But I want you to give me a call. You have my number, and you know how to get a hold of me. I want you to think this over for two days. The only help that you will get from this Bible study monetarily is rehab help. That's what I promise you. You're always welcome here on Monday nights. But we won't enable you to keep destroying your life. You have a choice to make."

But small is the gate and narrow the road that leads to life, and only a few find it.

—from the Gospel of Matthew

CHAPTER 31: CORNER

James made up his mind. There wasn't anything left to say. We all sat in the room, staring at the table. Bill finally got up and started to walk out.

"Let's go, Chris."

I looked up at Bill and decided to just follow him out the door. What else could I do? Brit got up as well and then James. Exiting the building, Brit softly said to James, "Hey, man, I'll give you a ride back to your corner."

"Thanks."

"I'll go with you," I said.

"Chris, my toiletries are still at your house."

"I'll go get them. I'll be right back," I said, thankful for the alone time. I jumped in my Saturn and drove a mile back to my gated driveway. I climbed the stairs and entered my apartment. The air was still colored by smelly feet. *At least I won't have that to deal with anymore.* That was a small consolation. I would live with his smelly feet every day if that would somehow bring about a change in his life.

I went into his room and grabbed the black toiletry bag that had his toothbrush and other personal hygiene items. I opened his black duffle bag and was about to stuff a blanket in it. I noticed his papers and other things. *Cover for drugs?* I leafed through James's stuff again. Papers, medical records, and magazines—nothing incriminating. At least James was honest about not being on drugs while he was here.

I finished stuffing the blanket into the large duffle bag and left the room. As I walked down the stairs, betrayal knotted my stomach. I tried not to think about it. I was still in reaction mode. *How could this happen? Why didn't I see it? Why doesn't he want help?* I made my way down to my car, put the bag in my trunk, and headed back to the seminary.

Only five days ago, I was celebrating the fact that James had a job and a future. Five days ago, God was answering prayers, and my sacrifice for James had paid off. He had steady income and a chance to make it. He was a walking testimonial for Jesus Christ. But tonight I learned that he'd been lying to me about being clean, about wanting to make a difference, about everything.

I pulled back into the Café Koine parking lot and drove up to James and Brit standing near Brit's SUV. Bill leaned against his car door and watched. I quickly got out and tossed James his bag of toiletries and then moved to the trunk for his duffle bag.

"Hey, guy, gimme a call after y'all drop him off. Just wanna make sure y'all are safe tonight," Bill said with genuine concern.

"Roger that. I'll call you in a bit."

I popped the trunk and grabbed James's duffle.

"Could you keep that for a while? I can't exactly sleep on the street tonight with my big bag. I need somewhere to put it," James said with no emotion.

"Yeah, I can do that." I put the bag back into the trunk and then walked over to Brit's Xterra.

James rode shotgun, and I climbed in the back seat. Brit started the SUV and headed toward downtown. As we drove through Deep Ellum, I wondered what would become of James. He looked over at Brit. "I'm thirsty. Can we stop at a 7-Eleven?"

"I don't have any money, bro," Brit replied. James looked at Brit's coin tray. Brit followed his gaze. "Hey, man, I've got about seventy cents."

"Here's a quarter," I chimed in. I handed the coin to James and again wondered what his response would be to these men who really cared for him.

We pulled into the 7-Eleven parking lot, and Brit and I waited while James went inside. For a moment, we sat in silence. Then Brit turned around.

"This is ministry, man. This is the real deal. You can't learn this from studying Hebrew," Brit said.

He was right. This was ministry and studying the Bible is important, but living it is far more important. Dr. Hoe had said that many students are like bad photographs: overexposed and underdeveloped. I can always use some more development, but this "development" didn't sit right in my soul.

"What about James, man? All this and we end up taking him back to a street corner. He can't even acknowledge that he's living a complete lie. I mean, look at him, Brit. He's in there getting a Coke and is just going through the motions, prepping to head back to life on the street. He doesn't care."

"Hey, bro, we're not responsible for James's reaction. But look what happened through this. We all became closer. James can never say that the church doesn't love him. We were the real church to him, Chris. We can only love him like Christ loved us. That's our role."

"I guess."

James crawled back into the SUV and sipped his Coke. We drove the rest of the way in silence until we finally arrived at the corner of St. Paul and Corsicana. The sidewalk was packed with homeless men settling in for the night. Some were talking, others were sleeping, and still others were intently looking our way. I got out and went to the back of Brit's vehicle to get James's toiletries. I handed over the bag and grabbed James's shoulder.

"Hey, man, let's pray," I said. James acquiesced.

I lifted my heart up to the Lord with a passion that God might change the situation and transform the death that was in James's heart to life. I prayed with all I had, while James stared past me, just watching those men sleeping along the sidewalk. *Oh well, at least God heard me.*

With that, I hugged James. He became a motionless mannequin. I let him go. He moved past me to the sidewalk to rejoin the population of the disheartened and disenfranchised. James looked like he was walking to his grave. I watched for a moment. It reminded me of watching James from the same angle as he was leaving Fellowship Church many months ago. Was this just a bad social experiment, or was this God working? I knew that I wouldn't give up on James; SPF7 wouldn't give up on James. But would James give up on James? I prayed not. There was still hope. There was always hope.

The Lord is not slow in keeping his promise, as some understand slowness. He is patient with you, not wanting anyone to perish, but everyone to come to repentance.

—from the Second Letter of Peter

CHAPTER 32: Silence

Tuesday morning came, and my careful watch of my cell phone didn't cause James to call. I went to the library and worked for six hours on a paper at my lonely cubicle. As much as I knew this Greek paper would further my understanding of Ephesians 5:22–33, my heart wasn't in it.

I didn't feel like talking to Brit or Bill or anyone else, for that matter. I wondered what James was thinking right now. Did he consider the fact that he had the whole world ahead of him for the taking if he was willing to accept it? Or was he content to wallow in a cycle of drug addiction that would lead him to another dozen hospital visits over the course of the next couple of months?

My hope started to wane. I wondered if his public failure would cause him to drown himself in crack and pain killers to get past the moment. I didn't know if he would ever call again, and Tuesday passed with no word.

Brit called. "Hey, bro, any word yet?"

"Nah, man. It might be too early to expect anything," I said.

"Yeah, you're probably right," Brit said.

"Did we do the right thing?"

"We did all we could do."

After another couple of minutes of small talk, I hung up the phone and took a nap.

Wednesday morning Greek class began with the usual call for prayer requests. I let them in on James's situation and asked them to pray for James to make the right decision. I'm not sure if it's okay to ask God to force someone to get his life together, but I put the request in, anyway. One of the guys prayed that James would come back and then asked the Lord for his help in finishing our Greek papers and that none of us would have to retake the class. Dr. Hoe then furthered our Greek education by dropping as many *Star Wars* analogies as possible in relating Greek paradigms to our current reality. They were about as cheesy as a block of Wisconsin cheddar, but it did help me remember the Greek and kept my attention somewhat. Dr. Hoe had his work cut out for him in competing for my focus. I vigilantly watched my cell phone in hopes that some random unknown number might pop up. But there were no texts, vibrations, or rings.

I spent Thursday at the library immersed in a Greek-English lexicon. I looked up words in first-century Greek and cross-referenced them with classical Greek, attempting to derive the origin of the word, which might in turn grant me a deeper understanding of the word "submitting." But even after several hours of study, it turns out the Greek word *hupotasso,* which is rendered "submit" in most translations of Ephesians 5:21, really means "submit." *Incredible.*

This tedious studying called for a break and a reason to think about James again. I called Bill to ask him what he thought.

"Guy, you know as well as I do, he ain't comin' back. Chris, you don't want him back. He won't change until it hurts bad enough. He's become such an expert at conning good people like you that he's biding his time to find another victim. That's how he operates."

"I really wanted this to be different, Bill," I managed. "I thought that if I prayed enough or sacrificed enough that it'd be enough."

"Chris, he still sees himself as the victim. Until that changes, he won't change. After the age of fifteen, nobody's a victim anymore. Everyone's gotta choice."

"Yeah, I guess you're right."

For being so ornery, Bill was actually pretty wise. His phrase "after the age of fifteen, nobody's a victim" was classic Bill. He said it so many times about people who complained or whined that sometimes I wondered if he overgeneralized it. However, there was something to be said about Bill's incredible accuracy. Still, I wanted him to be wrong. Isn't God's wisdom foolishness to the world?[1] Yet, a man has to want God's wisdom. I'm still not sure how that mystery transpires.

Thursday turned into Friday. Nothing.

I still had James's duffle bag, his HIV-positive magazines, and hospital records: his life-in-a-bag. I pulled it out one more time to look through the contents as if they would contain some new clue about why he hadn't called. *How long will this go on? What will it take to break James's cycle? Lord, intervene here.*

Michael Riley called, and his voice sounded concerned. "Chris, I went down to the DRC to feed the homeless. James was there. He said something about just telling you guys what you wanted to hear. I don't know what that was about, and I don't want to get into the middle of it, but I thought you should know."

"Yeah, that doesn't surprise me," I replied. "Are you still there?"

"No, I'm heading home now. He said he wanted his stuff back."

"Okay," I responded, put off by the fact that James didn't call me, but then I realized he had other issues he was trying to work through. I decided to let it go.

"What are you going to do?" he asked.

"I don't know, man," I said. "If you see him again, tell him he's still welcome at the Bible study."

"Okay, I will. I've already left, but next time if he's there, I'll tell him. Why didn't you come down here?"

"Man, I'm still working on Greek stuff. But next time if I'm free, I'll be there."

I wondered what God was doing within the silence of James. He had my number but hadn't called. This evening he hid behind another lie to fend off Michael Riley's questioning. I'm learning not to be surprised by that. The natural course of the human spirit is to cover up. That has been happening since the garden of Eden. God caught Adam and Eve redhanded, wearing their fig-leaf best, but they never confessed their sin. God gave them grace anyway. Should I have just taken James back anyway, like Christ would have? Or was that a spiritual matter for Jesus, and I was to push him into his arms by kicking him out of my home. What were we supposed to do as "James's church"? What should I do as the guy who took some ownership and responsibility for his life? How am I supposed to handle this? *God, give me some answers.*

Suppose one of you has a hundred sheep and loses one of them. Does he not leave the ninety-nine in the open country and go after the lost sheep until he finds it? And when he finds it . . . he calls his friends and neighbors together and says, "Rejoice with me; I have found my lost sheep." I tell you that in the same way there will be more rejoicing in heaven over one sinner who repents than over ninety-nine righteous persons who do not need to repent.

—from the Gospel of Luke

CHAPTER 33: PATROL

Monday finally came, and SPF7 gathered once again at the President's Room of Café Koine. The awkwardness of last week didn't change the fact that we came here to have the gospel poured out over our lives to transform our mere existence into life-changing purpose.

After the Bible study ended, I asked my men to huddle up and pray. We don't usually do the praying-while-touching thing, but that night it just felt right. I asked God to protect us as we went down to search for James to give him back his stuff. We knew it might be a fruitless enterprise, but we had to try. I also hoped James might be overwhelmed by the love of several men looking for him out on the streets.

I could see it happening, like a movie playing in my head. The men from SPF7 would be walking the streets, surrounded by the homeless, to bring love to one man who felt rejected by all society. I could see it so clearly—all of us wrapping our arms around James and asking him to come home and get rehab, James crying in repentance, accepting with tears and disbelief that we loved him that much.

After praying I took volunteers to join me in the search for James. Bill, Scott-Michael, Brit, and Michael Riley decided to go down there with me. I went to my car, grabbed James's bag from the trunk, and headed toward Brit's SUV. I gave the men a situation report of what we could expect from the homeless population and briefed them on our mission: spot and drop. Find James, give him his stuff, and then, if possible, extract him to rehab. I detailed our route, what to do in case things went bad, ensured everyone was armed with cell phones and numbers, and asked questions of the other drivers, Michael Riley and Scott-Michael, to make sure they understood the plan. We then mounted our vehicles.

It felt for a moment like being in Habbaniyah, Iraq, about to roll into sector on mission. I'd be standing in my tank getting a "good to go" from my driver, loader, and gunner. I'd slap a fresh magazine into my M-4 carbine rifle, charge it, and place it next to my .50-caliber machine gun. Placing the .50-cal ammo in the feed tray, I'd slam the cover down and pull back on the charging handle, feeling the round seating itself into position. I'd look over at my wingman, First Lieutenant Rob Kessel in his Bradley, and give him a thumbs-up. He would smile and signal back. Giving my driver the command to "move out," I'd motion for Rob to follow me. Sometimes we'd head off to a battle. Sometimes we'd investigate a shooting. Sometimes we'd go to my informant Omar's house. Every time we left, the smell of jet fuel used in the 1600-horse-power turbine engine would invigorate my soul and make my pulse quicken for battle.

That same feeling swept over me as Michael Riley pulled his car behind us and Scott-Michael mounted his motorcycle. After getting a thumbs-up from everyone, I led the way in Brit's Xterra toward "the corner," watching my rearview mirror closely to make sure no one got lost.

I dreaded playing *Where's Waldo?* searching for James among the throngs of people. As we maneuvered through tall buildings, I silently prayed that God would make James very apparent to us. I prayed that there would be no trouble, no violence, and no fear. I prayed that when we found James, it wouldn't be awkward.

No one spoke a word.

Turning down Cadiz we saw the typical scenery of homeless men littering the streets. Many unashamed slept on the sidewalk. It was difficult to discern who was who, but we knew James's figure by now. We made one lap around "the corner," but no one spotted him. I decided to go for another lap. No sign of him. I stopped the car for a moment and just watched. I flashed back to that moment over a month ago looking for James to pick him up and take him home. Now I was looking to give him his stuff back. It felt like a bad breakup.

Scott-Michael rode his motorcycle over to a homeless man who was awake. I watched him take off his helmet and motion with his hands, trying to describe James. The man shook his head and held out his hand for a dollar. Scott-Michael obliged. We still had no idea where James was. I wondered if he was getting high again somewhere or if he just was simply not there. *But where else would he be—the crack house in the 'hood?*

I wanted to be an ambassador of Christ. I wanted to show the world that the church really does look after its family and how the power of Christ has transformed us to love those whom the world has rejected.

I wondered if James would spin the story of us helping him into another rejection story like all the others. But that wasn't my problem. I couldn't control that, and more importantly I couldn't even find James to show him the love of our Savior.

Scott-Michael rode over to me. "Hey, man, he isn't here. No one knows where he is."

"We tried. I don't know what else we can do."

"We can come back again sometime," Scott-Michael replied.

"Yeah, I guess," I said defeated. "If I could remember where that one crack house was, we could go there."

"Maybe he'll call us."

"I doubt it," I said, staring at the homeless men behind Scott-Michael.

"Sorry, man."

"It's all right; let's go home," I said as my ambitious resolution to find James waned.

We drove back to the seminary and talked briefly about "trying" and "doing all we could do" and "James has to want to change" and a whole bunch of jargon that sat empty on the asphalt. *This isn't the way it's supposed to be.*

I went home and climbed into my loft bed.

God, do something.

Dear friend, I pray that you may enjoy good health and that all may go well with you, even as your soul is getting along well.

—from the Third Letter of John

CHAPTER 34: E-MAIL

Wednesday morning came, and I slept in. I had turned in my Greek final paper a couple of days previous and now was free from class until the last week of August. I rejoiced as eleven o'clock rolled around, and I still hadn't gotten out of bed. *Oh, the life of a student.*

I decided to go for a run. Sweat cascaded down my back the moment I walked out of my apartment. It was almost a hundred degrees outside, but the trees in the median of Swiss Avenue provided shade and reminded me of running in similar conditions in Iraq. We were stationed right by the Euphrates River, and the high water table provided ample supply for gorgeous trees to line the roads of our army base.

I finished my run, came home, showered, and sat for ten minutes, enjoying a moment of nothingness. I picked up my Bible and read through Matthew in preparation for the next week's Bible study and wondered whether the deal with James would rock or invigorate anyone's faith.

That's when it came. An e-mail from James showed up on my phone, but for some reason it wouldn't download. A quick shot of adrenaline mixed with impatience hit me as I waited for my dial-up connection to download the message to my laptop so I could read it. Okay, I know what you're thinking, *Dial-up?* But it is dial-up because it goes through my Verizon cell phone, which is tethered to my computer, and the speed is dial-up, not DSL. The reliability of my Internet reminds me of the old-school modems.

From: James Rudolph, Jr.
Sent: Wednesday, August 15, 2007 3:12 PM
To: Chris Plekenpol

Subject: James's Stuff

Hey,
I hear that you guys came to the corner of Corsicana and St. Paul twice. Well, I was there. So how about I be there as I usually am Thursday and Friday and see if we can hook up!! I really need my Bible. I'll be there after 9 pm because that is usually when it is most convenient for you!! If you get this message today, I'll be there tonight after 9 pm as I always am. Hope that this will not be a problem.
James

I wondered if he had really been there or if that was all just a little story. I mean, if he was there, why wouldn't he come up and say something? What was he waiting for? Or if he was asleep, why wouldn't someone wake him up? James had lied before; how was this any different? Lying is just what he did. Maybe I'd become jaded, or maybe I understood the streets a little better now. The streets cause people to lie as a way of life. I didn't want to think of him as a liar, but there it was. Sin takes over slowly, but eventually it consumes the heart. I decided to write James back.

From: Chris Plekenpol
Sent: Wednesday, August 15, 2007 4:48 PM
To: James Rudolph, Jr.

Subject: RE: James's Stuff

James, I'm looking forward to it. I'll bring it by tonight at nine.
See you then, brother!
If you can, let me know how you are doing.
In Him,
Chris

Driving down to "the corner" alone wouldn't be wise. I needed a compadre bold enough to venture down there and help me find James. I figured we'd have to get out of the car and make a personal call on the men of St. Paul and Corsicana. I also needed someone compassionate enough to love him where he was and perhaps invite him to go to rehab or Celebrate Recovery for his addiction. I knew

Brit had a dinner party that his wife was putting on with some business associates of hers. I also knew that Brit had no desire whatsoever to be there and would be looking for an outlet to escape the tedium of an Arbonne International meeting. Sharpening my persuasive skills, I called to tell Brit of our impending mission.

"Brit, when are you done tonight with your wife's thing?"

"I don't know, bro. Who knows how long these things will go? I'm just trying to have a good attitude."

"Nice. I got an e-mail from James," I said.

"What'd he say?"

"He wants me to bring his stuff down to 'the corner.' You coming?" I asked.

"I've got this thing going on."

"Come on, Brit. There are a million more of those things you can go to."

"I know; let me check with Ash. She probably won't mind. Hold on." I listened and tried to overhear Brit ask his wife if he could come out tonight with me. *Married people.* I felt like I was calling my best friend in fifth grade, Matt Goller, to see if his mom would let him come out and play.

"Hey, bro, I can go after the Arbonne thing, at like nine," Brit said.

"Cool; call me whenever you're done with your little dinner party."

"Who else is going?" he asked with a tinge of nervousness.

"Just us."

"Is it safe?" he asked.

"It's never safe, but it is good," I responded tongue in cheek and with a C. S. Lewis allusion—the one about Aslan.

"Okay, I'll call you."

I'd wanted to get down to "the corner" right at nine o'clock. Getting there too late would be asking for trouble. But I also wanted Brit to go with me, and he was the only one who could fit this adventure into his schedule and who also had the perfect demeanor for James in this condition. I checked my cell phone continuously, starting at eight forty-five to make sure I hadn't missed any calls.

At nine thirty Brit finally called and told me he "would be there soon," which meant that I had about fifteen minutes. *Better late than never.* I quickly shoved the remnants of my dinner, a tasty oatmeal raisin Clif Bar, into my mouth, put some dishes in the sink, and then grabbed James's life-in-a-bag. I had hoped to get down there before it got too late, but maybe the later we left, the more apt we would be to walk among the sleeping homeless undetected.

I walked down the stairs of my apartment and out to the curb to wait for Brit. The night was hot. If I stayed out there for too long, I would start to sweat. But there was no rain, and I was grateful for that. Brit's SUV turned onto my street, and he pulled up to my curb. Brit gave me a surfer nod as I moved toward the back of his vehicle to put James's bag inside.

A friend loves at all times,
and a brother is born for adversity.

—from the Book of Proverbs

CHAPTER 35: SEARCH

"I'm not so sure I feel comfortable about getting out of the truck," Brit said.

"Who says we're going to need to get out?" I asked.

"I don't know. I haven't been to combat, so this isn't exactly comfortable. I don't want to do anything stupid. I have a wife, you know."

"That's fair. Nothing stupid," I promised him.

Brit slid me a sandwich that he'd made for me across the dashboard of the SUV. I think he felt sorry for me because all I ever ate was Café Brazil, and married life had afforded him the luxury of eating home-cooked meals. I'm not sure how a sandwich made at

Brit's house was any better than a sandwich from Café Brazil, but I did appreciate not eating alone.

Brit's anxiety about going into the streets to search for James started to build in me as well. I ate my sandwich in silence as I mentally prepared for our two-man reconnaissance mission for James. Maybe tonight with fewer people we wouldn't stick out quite so bad and attract unwanted attention. However, I did prefer having numbers on my side just in case something went down. I had contemplated grabbing my Colt .45 from my dresser and heading to the streets armed but felt that might cause more problems than it would solve.

I finished my sandwich as we made another turn down toward "the corner." I remembered many times pacing about in Brit's kitchen, trying to figure out whether I should take James in. It wasn't that long ago that I'd been there. I knew it hadn't been a failure, but there wasn't much left to say about it now. We'd exhausted our conversation topics, so I sat wondering what James was thinking and what he might say to us when we saw him tonight. At least it could be in our favor that Bill wasn't coming, which might soften James's mood toward us.

God, please change his heart.

I wanted God to force James to get his act together. At this point, he had no ability to be responsible for himself. He was hooked on drugs, and he desperately needed God to intervene. Or maybe he hadn't hit rock bottom yet. Bill always said that's when people change, when it hurts enough. He always told me that James didn't hurt enough yet.

"You ready?" Brit turned the vehicle onto Cadiz and fingered the keys in the ignition. He smiled at me in my moment of contemplation.

"Yeah, let's do this. This is going be good." I smiled.

"Most def, bro."

"Do you want to pray?" I asked.

"Sure, bro. Go for it." Brit pulled the Xterra over by the DRC, and I led us in prayer.

"Lord," I started, "make James be down here tonight. Don't let us drive around forever and come up empty-handed. Help James be responsive when we see him and change his heart that he would want help. Don't let our love for James be in vain. In Jesus' name, amen."

Brit looked over at me for a moment and then got the Xterra moving again.

"Are you thinking that any of this has been a waste?"

"I'm trying not to," I said. "I know in my head that God is in control and sovereign, but what good is any of this if we don't see James change?"

"That isn't it at all."

"It isn't? I mean Bill was right all along," I said.

"I'll be the first to tell you that I didn't see this coming. But if you look at this as a complete failure, you're being kinda selfish," Brit stated, cutting his eyes toward me.

I looked at Brit like he was crazy, but I had learned over the past several months that I'm wrong about things more often than I care to admit. I figured I'd hear him out on this.

"You're looking at this like you did James some big favor, and he didn't pay you back. I don't know about you, but having him over for dinner really opened my eyes to the reality of the hell of being on the streets. He is going back to a sidewalk, bro. He has no concept of what it is for someone to love him without getting something in return. That's the way of the streets. Everything is earned."

"So, what about all the stuff we gave him?" I asked.

"Well, even that was conditional." Brit looked at me as we pulled up to a stoplight.

"What are we supposed to do, keep feeding his habit?"

"No, we're doing the right thing. He needs to trust the only One who will never fail him and who has the power to change him and love him through this. We can't do that. That job belongs to God."

"I guess," I said unconvinced.

"Did James do anything redeeming the whole time he was with you?"

"Yeah, the time he whined about not going to Six Flags, he totally turned it around and gave some of the most godly, awesome advice I'd ever heard to Kevin and talked to him about the consequences of being gay, the pain of drugs, and all that. I see your point, Brit; I get it. But didn't you think there would be something more?"

"There will be. We just see things in snapshots."

"Huh?" I asked.

"Take my cell phone cam, for instance. If I take a pic of you here, it shows you, being frustrated. It doesn't show the fact that we are on a big adventure to give James another shot at life. There's always more to the picture. We're only seeing part of it. But what I know is that God sees everything played out simultaneously in HD. He can see this moment along with the ten other times James receives his grace from someone else trying to be the hands and feet of Jesus. He also sees how this has shaped you for your future ministry opportunities. Pretty much, this ranks up there with a gaping barrel off Honolua Bay."

I let that thought settle and wondered what exactly a "gaping barrel" was.

"Hey, bro, you see him?" Brit interjected. I looked left and right. The homeless were sprawled out on the sidewalk, and a man with bulging bright white eyes stared at us.

"No, where're you looking?"

"Everywhere, bro."

"Oh, I thought you saw him," I said, continuing to look.

We continued to scan the homeless. Everyone looked the same. If James was here, he was an incredible illusionist.

"Do you want to get out of the car?" I looked at Brit.

"Bro," he protested.

"We don't have to; I'm just saying if we're going look for him, let's look for him."

"What's the difference between us driving slowly and walking slowly?"

"We don't have to," I conceded.

"Thanks."

"Park over there for a second, and let's just watch and see if we can see something," I said.

We drove the Xterra a block down from "the corner" and watched. I felt like we were on some sort of stakeout. Although we felt incognito, Brit's SUV stuck out in the 'hood, like a luxury vehicle with a couple of preppy white guys in it. "The corner" started to take notice of us.

"Bro, I don't see him."

"I don't either. I just don't want to get another e-mail telling me how we drove by twice and he was here. Let's give it a sec."

We waited, and several holey-shirted men with beards and hollow faces turned our direction and stared.

"Bro, if he's here, then he may be intentionally trying to set us up."

"What happened to 'this is our snapshot and God sees everything in HD'?"

"Bro, if he was here, he would have come up to us by now. We've been sitting here for twenty minutes."

"More like ten, but you're right. Let's take one more lap and then call it a night."

We drove around the block once again. The men who were awake threw up their hands up in exasperation as if we had just driven an SUV through their living room. We drove around the block, down to city hall, through the side streets near the library—plenty of homeless people, but no James.

"Bro, we've done all we can tonight. Let's take it to the house," Brit said.

"Roger."

Whatever you have learned or received or heard from me, or seen in me—put it into practice. And the God of peace will be with you.

—from the Letter to the Philippians

CHAPTER 36: CHUCK

Every new semester at Dallas Seminary starts the same. I like the regularity. Our chancellor, Chuck Swindoll, always comes the first week, and the DTS Chapel is packed. I actually have to jockey for position to get my usual front-and-center seat. Many hapless students sit on the floor or stand in the lobby and lean in, trying to glean Swindoll's wisdom. He gives us different Scriptures but usually comes around to saying the same thing every August or January. I love it every time as the message speaks right to me. Here's the *Cliffs Notes* version of every one of Chuck's seminary messages:

1. You will never face more spiritual attack than you will at seminary.

2. Sometimes the most spiritual thing you can do is take a nap.

3. Make deep friendships. Seminary, and ministry in general, is a lonely place.

4. Forgive, forgive. Forgive, because eventually you'll need someone to forgive you.

I've heard the message repeatedly, but it never gets old. Dr. Swindoll has a special place in my heart, which makes me a little biased.

When I first came to Christ in 1999, I didn't have a clue who to listen to or how to get more Bible knowledge and grow spiritually. I did whatever I could, and usually that meant listening to the radio. During my lunch breaks at Fort Bragg, I would sit in my Chevy Blazer and listen to Chuck Swindoll and Tony Evans preach. I remember asking a friend where those guys learned to preach like that. The answer was Dallas Theological Seminary, and since then I have been a DTS fanatic.

When seminary started for me in 2006, Dr. Swindoll came to preach, and I went to introduce myself to him. I could feel the emotion rising as I went to meet the man whom I had never seen before but who was primarily responsible for my early Christian growth. I handed him my book, *Faith in the Fog of War,* and didn't get two words out before I started bawling. I mean really crying—little-kid-sobbing-style. It was so embarrassing. He asked me if the war had been too much. I was so embarrassed that the reason I was crying was not because of posttraumatic stress caused by combat, but because Chuck Swindoll meant so much to me. I nodded and buried my tears in his shoulder. He hugged me hard and said something pastoral.

So, as Chuck shared his regular message on this day, I smiled to myself with that memory and nodded at the truths he issued once again. I started to wish James could hear this message. Maybe that would change him.

Catching myself projecting Chuck's message onto James, I stopped and thought instead about how it affected me. Number one: seminary had definitely been a place of profound spiritual attack. I had many a person warn me before coming here that I needed to be careful and not let my spiritual life "die at *cemetery.*" My spiritual life has suffered, but not because of seminary. Anytime you pour yourself day after day into rigorous academics, your spiritual life is bound to suffer because we Americans value the urgent—turning in papers and earning a good grade.[1] The important—spending time with God—gets relegated to leftovers. I'm no different.

Number two: I haven't slept much these past several years, and a nap would probably do me good, as soon as I knock out the next exegetical.

Number three: seminary has been a lonely place, but those who have stuck the closest to me, Bill and Brit, haven't shirked their responsibility of friendship. Bill went out of his way to care for me. Brit gave himself, heart and soul, to the cause. Without them, I doubt I would have ever considered anything like taking James home. I wondered if I've been diligent to return the favor.

Finally, I'd forgiven James, repeatedly. And now with my apartment no longer carrying the pungent odor of his feet, I didn't have to grimace every time I walked in the door. The day that I aired out my apartment didn't win me any points with my landlords next door. They had a hard time with me opening up all the windows and blasting the air conditioning. I decided that my best course of action would be to give a simple apology and not try to explain the situation. The less they knew about the whole thing, the better.

Yes, forgiving James had been easier than expected. I think it starts with recognizing that I have really hurt some people myself and then understanding that Christ has forgiven me, despite my best efforts to ruin his name.

I also have a deeper understanding now of drug addiction and how it completely controlled James to the point that Christ became just a good idea to him. I have a million private sins that are not as destructive and are not as noticeable and yet break the heart of God. Am I really any different?

I let Dr. Swindoll's message penetrate, and when he came to the summation of what grace really means, he wept. I wept too. Hearing him talk, I couldn't help going back to the days right after my salvation when I couldn't escape the wonder of being made new. This doesn't make sense to someone who has never experienced it, but it's so amazing in those first couple of days when you realize that God really does love you, mess and all. In fact, I hadn't changed anything outwardly when he started loving me. And in all reality, I'm not that much different from what I was almost ten years ago. Yet, he loves me.

When chapel ended, I sat there and let the place empty and watched Dr. Swindoll wade through the line of adoring students who hoped for a handshake and a personal word of encouragement.

That chapel message put me in the right frame of mind to head off to Nashville, where I would enter the prisons again. I went to class and then home to pack up my army pants, Ranger T-shirt, beret, and boots—standard uniform for going into the prisons. I prayed for James as I zipped closed my suitcase and ventured to the airport.

For if you forgive men when they sin against you, your heavenly Father will also forgive you. But if you do not forgive men their sins, your Father will not forgive your sins.

—from the Gospel of Matthew

CHAPTER 37: Call

A couple of weeks and a lot of homework later, I found myself heading to my home away from home to enliven my study time. It was a Friday night, and Café Brazil was buzzing. I felt slightly awkward bringing in homework, wearing T-shirt and shorts, while all of SMU were wearing their clubbin' clothes, dressed to impress. I sat down at my favorite corner table and only felt slightly guilty for hogging a four-top while a line of potential clientele waited outside.

The smell of Brazilian burgers, coffee, and inebriated college students saturated the air. I liked this atmosphere most nights, but tonight I was tired. Instead of working on Romans, I surfed Facebook and eavesdropped on the guy with the spiky hair, sport coat, and ripped jeans talking about how much Miller he had just bonged.

Work wasn't going to get done on this night. It wasn't the distractions. That was normal. But rather, I felt worn down from the excitement and highs and lows of what James and seminary had brought into my life. So, after spending an hour and a half wasting time, I packed up my laptop and books and headed for my Saturn. My cell phone rang as I threw everything in the back seat of the car. I answered; it was Michael Riley.

"Hey, I'm feeding the homeless down here at the DRC."

Immediately I felt guilty, as if that's where I should be. I shook it off and responded, "That's great, man; what's going on down there?"

"James is here. He looks kind of pissed off. He wants his stuff back."

"Great. Tell him to stay there. I'm on my way. Don't let him leave your sight."

When I was in Nashville a few weeks ago, Michael Riley had called and said the same thing. James was upset that I wouldn't give him his stuff back—like I was holding it hostage. Michael Riley informed me of the deal, and I intended to go down and check the DRC on Friday nights, as I'd been accustomed to doing, but traveling and speaking and homework happen, and the DRC falls from the frontal lobe.

Needless to say, I headed back to my apartment and ran up the stairs. I grabbed the duffle bag from beside the coffee table and sprinted back down to the Saturn. I drove as fast as I could to the DRC, not wanting to miss James again. Turning on Cadiz, I saw the familiar chain link guarding the DRC. I spotted Michael Riley, sunglasses on top of his head, carrying on a conversation with a droopy homeless man who could only be James.

I parked the car and hopped out. Adrenaline swelled through my veins, and I felt a rush of emotion. My smile spanned ear to ear as I looked James in the face. He didn't return the joy. Without regard to personal boundary space, I hugged him. James remained as stiff as a mannequin.

"Hey, man, how've you been?" I asked.

"I'm okay. Same thing. I got a job but got fired again."

James was playing his victim card, but this wasn't the time to confront him.

"Sorry, man," I managed.

He explained briefly his experiences at different jobs. Either a job wasn't the right fit or the ID scandal still affected his search. Both issues continued to haunt him. He had stayed with different people, but they had all turned out to be liars and cheats. I was surprised that he'd even had one job, but I didn't question it. I just let him talk.

His mannerisms hadn't changed. Although still droopy and never making eye contact, he articulated everything clearly and without pause. As he spoke, I wondered how much actual truth was coming out of his mouth. My inner monologue started screaming, *Liar, liar, pants on fire!* I watched for the indicators of either lying or drug use that Bill had taught me. He looked fine—and droopy.

"You got my stuff?" James asked abruptly, capping his talk on his recent struggles. "I really need my Bible."

"Yeah, I got it." I went to the back of my car and pulled out the duffle bag and handed it to him. He pulled on the zippers and briefly went through it, ensuring all contents were there.

"Thanks," he said without emotion.

I didn't know what else to say. I looked at James and saw that same hardness that had been his modus operandi the whole time I knew him. He'd allowed me to see a soft spot that one time after I picked him up from the hospital at four in the morning. But there was no "thanks" in James tonight.

"Hey, James." I observed his eyes searching the ground for a place other than my face to look. "You know you can always come back to SPF7. There is no judgment there. We all still love you, and there are no hard feelings."

James glanced up for a moment and then looked back down.

"Look, man, do you need anything?" I asked sincerely.

James paused, and I thought he would say nothing. "Yeah, I do. I need some deodorant, toothpaste, and mouthwash," he managed.

"Come Monday night, and I'll take care of you."

"Maybe. I dunno."

"Come on, man, what else do you have to do? No obligation, brother. You don't have to go to rehab or do anything like that; just come back and hang with us, and I'll give you a hygiene hookup," I said.

"Okay, maybe."

"I'll take a maybe; that's not a 'no,'" I said. But inside, I knew it was a "no." James had made his decision and was sticking with it.

Michael Riley interjected, "Hey, man, come on back. We do miss you."

"I know. I know. I'll think about it."

And those were the last words I remember James saying. He would think about it. There wasn't much to think about. Either he would come on Monday or he would spend the night on the streets, smelly armpits and all, potentially getting in trouble with the law or with someone else. But I couldn't make that call for him.

Three days later Monday came as it always did. I brought the Listerine, toothpaste, and deodorant just in case—but that didn't make him show.

His malice may be concealed by deception,
but his wickedness will be exposed in the assembly.

If a man digs a pit, he will fall into it;
if a man rolls a stone, it will roll back on him.

A lying tongue hates those it hurts,
and a flattering mouth works ruin.

—from the Book of Proverbs

CHAPTER 38: LIAR

A lonely, plastic Wal-Mart bag fully stocked with hygiene items sat in the back seat of my Saturn for days. I didn't have the heart to take it into my apartment and use it as my own. Every time I considered bringing it up, I would leave it in the back seat, hoping that I might somehow see James again.

On Friday evening I glanced in the back of my Saturn, and instead of heading home, I drove over to the DRC. It was packed because on this particular night the kind folks from Northwest Bible Church again brought clothing along with the meal they served. These nights were extremely popular since shoes and pants are a huge draw for the homeless as the colder months approached.

I decided to ask around to see if anyone had heard of James. One man stuck out as being particularly obnoxious and talkative. He sat in his wheelchair, reeking of alcohol, being loud and very profane. His shoulder-length blond hair was scraggly about his face, looking for a place to settle. The F-bomb seemed to be the only adjective in his repertoire. The guy was even a bit much for someone like me who had spent the last decade in the army.

He had an interesting sense of style for a homeless, wheelchair-bound guy, as his green button-up dress shirt oddly matched his shoes. His white pants, soiled by a lot of wear and not a lot of washing, complemented the outfit nicely. He also wore a scarf around his neck like a fashionable Dallas woman. Not that homeless people can't color-coordinate, but usually that's the last thing on a homeless dude's mind who has a limited wardrobe selection.

I held out my hand in front of his face. "I'm Chris."

He looked at my hand for a moment, as if deciding whether it was worthy to shake. I must have passed his examination because he grabbed it and shook it violently. He told me his name, which to this day I can't remember. I affectionately recall him as "the F-bomber."

"Hey, man, do you have a smoke on you?"

"I don't smoke, sorry. How are things going for you out here?"

"Oh, not too bad." His wheelchair started to roll toward the street, but he didn't seem to notice. I grabbed the chair, preventing him from darting into traffic.

"Whoa, man, you all right?"

"****, I'm fine, nothin' a shot of Jack and a smoke won't cure. You got a smoke?"

"No, I don't, sorry." At this point, I usually would have turned and walked away and gone back to the group, but something about this guy made me linger.

"You got any family?" I asked, trying to be conversational. But he looked like he didn't hear me or was in his own world.

"Where are you staying tonight?" I asked him. He smiled really big, and his eyes got wide. *Creepy.*

"Oh, I know people. They take good care of me, because I take good care of them," he cackled.

The conversation had just turned a shade of weird, which I didn't feel like investigating. I started to turn, but he grabbed my wrist.

"Hey, you got a dollar?"

"No, man, what do you need a dollar for? There's food right here." I stood there awkwardly and chalked this guy up to be mentally ill. "Hey, quick question. Do you know a guy named James?"

After I asked the question, I felt stupid because, honestly, of all the hundreds of homeless people who hang out here at the DRC, what are the odds? But I couldn't suck the words back into my mouth, so I waited for his answer.

"I know James," he said.

"You do? He's a black, heavyset guy, gap between the teeth," I added.

"I know James," he said again with resolution, his blue eyes looked through me as if caught in a memory.

"How do you know him?" I asked, questioning his integrity.

"James is gay, right?" he stated more than asked. I was dumbfounded.

"Yeah, he is. How do you know him?"

"James and I have done a few tricks together. We know each other—supposed to look out for each other, but not James. He's a selfish son of a *****."

"What? I thought James gave up that lifestyle," I said, wanting at least some of James's story to be true.

The F-bomber then went into detail about the tricks that James and he had pulled and how male prostitution was a means to an end of getting the next drug or next high. He went on about how James used people. He told me that James had stolen, lied, and did essentially every dirty thing imaginable. I didn't believe all of it. Although extreme exaggeration was a part of his colorful vernacular, something told me this guy wasn't completely off. He clearly knew James, and the things he said started to line up with the evidence I had observed over the past several weeks. *Was James prostituting himself when he went to do laundry?* I wanted to take a scalding hot shower.

I thanked the F-bomber for his time and wheeled him to the chow line. I even shared Christ with him, and his answer surprised me.

"I'm going to heaven. I know that Jesus died on the cross for my sins and rose from the dead," he said with such startling confidence that I made a face. "I'm in. Can't nobody judge me."

I decided not to push it as a couple more F-bombs fell out of his mouth, making a splash on those around us. He was beginning to wear me out, so I dropped it. Security forced me to part with my potty-mouthed friend. They were making people leave the area as the DRC was closing; the Northwest Bible Church people prayed over everyone and then called it a night. I went to my car, sat for a moment, and called Bill.

Bill wasn't surprised, but then, he never was. I called Brit, expecting him to be shocked, but he resonated more with Bill.

I well remember them,
and my soul is downcast within me.

Yet this I call to mind
and therefore I have hope:

Because of the Lord's great love we are not consumed,
for his compassions never fail.

They are new every morning;
great is your faithfulness.

—from the Book of Lamentations

CHAPTER 39: DRIVE

I hung up the phone with Brit and stared at the DRC. The main floodlights had been turned off, leaving only the security lights on for its own protection. The chain-link gate had been locked, and the security guard had shooed away the lingering patrons. I put the Saturn in gear and lurched away from the DRC, the F-bomber's words still fresh in my mind. I turned right on St. Paul Street and gave one final drive-by to "the corner." I didn't recognize anyone distinctly, but the old crew was there to enjoy another night on the sidewalk. I drove around the block and found more people under lit stairwells of old abandoned buildings. Like moths to flame, homeless people congregated under the lights. I later understood that was because the light was safer.

The light is always safer.

I turned onto Young Street and drove between the library and city hall. These two imposing buildings represented things the poor generally didn't have: knowledge and justice. Yet day after day you could find the homeless loitering about in and around both buildings. I drove down the alley behind the library and again passed person after person bedding down for the night under small door lamps. One slight man held my gaze for a moment as he pulled on his skullcap. I looked away.

I didn't have a late-night sermon on the radio to fill my mind; I let the city lights dance upon my windshield, and I listened to the urban sounds. Only one or two other vehicles passed by me. This part of town generally didn't see a lot of traffic at this hour. I drove past the Farmers' Market, which I decided was the invisible line between the haves and have-nots.

On the right side of the tracks the city bustled. I pulled up to an intersection and let a handful of people dressed to party walk across the street in front of me. I looked away from the red stoplight to the neon lights of the club scene. Outside Club Purgatory, young Dallasites and those who wished to see and be seen waited in a line that stretched around the corner, hoping for a chance to pay twenty dollars to enter the scene. The women wore Manolo's, Gucci, and Prada heels that looked sexy but extremely uncomfortable. I watched several men working their fingers through their three-hundred-dollar T-shirts, hoping to make the women believe that they had wealth, if only for the night. Such was the dilemma of the thirty-thousand-dollar millionaire. The clothes on the backs of those I could see standing outside the club could have put a heavy dent in the poverty in Dallas. But then, could the poor receive it?

I pulled my gaze from the partygoers, who had no clue that someone may have spied them with a tinge of frustration at their mindless search for pleasure. James could be in that group as well, on his futile search for fulfillment in illegal substances. Or maybe he was in a gay bar in the Oak Lawn area, "the gayborhood," pulling another trick for a high. A Rolodex of questions circulated through my mind on the whereabouts of James and his motivations. I couldn't stop at any one of them. No answers, just questions.

I turned the corner and drove past a lonely security guard walking by the granite block that said, "Touching Lives with Scripture." Seeing the night watchman working the graveyard shift of the vacant seminary reminded me that the people of faith were at home—or perhaps at Café Brazil.

I continued on past the massive houses on Swiss Avenue and turned into my driveway. I hit the gate opener and waited for the wrought-iron bars to welcome me home.

As I was sitting in the living room, my eyes fell on the spot where James used to sleep. No one noticed or cared that a man had totally thrown away a shot at success and getting on his feet. Business ran as usual from uptown to downtown, from the 'hood to the seminary—everyone carving out his or her piece of the pie, without a care that someone had thrown it all away.

Depravity is one of those theological concepts that doesn't make sense until you see it. I saw it in Iraq after finding four dead men in the back of a pickup truck, bullet holes in their foreheads and brain matter scattered throughout the truck bed. Their faces had been veiled with blood, and they smelled—dead. That's when the depravity of humanity started to make sense to me. They had been executed at point-blank range for telling American soldiers where roadside bombs were located. Their brothers were taking them to their burial place when I discovered them. It's hard to imagine how people get to a place where violence makes enough sense to kill people like that.

You've seen it on the news, too—a mother drowns her children in the bathtub or a father kills his wife and baby and then himself because he lost his job. Everyone's depravity affects him or her differently, but the problem is we're all depraved. I guess that's why no one is surprised when James doesn't change. When he rejects help, he does what any depraved person would do; he rejects the very thing that might save him.

I don't know if Christ had changed James's heart. I still don't understand the mystery of what happens to a person when Christ shows up in that person's life and becomes his or her all in all. I don't have to look too far past my own skin to realize sometimes God's grace isn't enough, because I still do the very things I don't want to do.

Paul, the New Testament writer, talked about that in Romans 7. He was a guy who planted more churches, suffered more for his faith, and was a master of the Bible. Even though he had all those strengths, he still struggled with sin. He said that he wanted to do good. His inner man, his soul, his very being wanted to do the right thing, but he lacked the power to carry it out. He said that even he didn't understand what he did. The very good that he wanted to do, he couldn't do it, but instead he did the very thing he hated.[1] He had to rely daily on Christ, and to do anything else would mean to live in his depravity.

The only difference between James and me is that I'm learning not to try to make it on my own. I have learned to just fail and fall into the arms of Jesus. That's how God's grace is enough. He forgives me, and, more than that, he is a better high. He is a better love. He is flat out better. I wish James could experience that. Jesus is better than fame, women, and cars. I wish those kids outside Purgatory could see that. Jesus is better than my own drive to be a successful Christian author, speaker, or pastor. And yet sometimes I feel that the other stuff is all there is; therefore, I can commiserate with those hapless souls outside Purgatory and underneath the street lamps on St. Paul and Corsicana. C. S. Lewis, one of my favorite authors, said something to this effect: "We're half-hearted creatures, fooling about with drink and sex and ambition when infinite joy is offered us, like an ignorant child who wants to go on making mud pies in a slum because he cannot imagine what is meant by the offer of a holiday at the sea. We're far too easily pleased."[2]

God, I don't want to be easily pleased.

Religion that God our Father accepts as pure and faultless is this: to look after orphans and widows in their distress and to keep oneself from being polluted by the world.

—from the Letter of James

EPiloGuE

Sometimes I think I didn't do enough for James. I remember that night at the seminary when we told James he couldn't live with me anymore, and I keep thinking, *What if I took him home again anyway?* Maybe he would be able to see God's unfailing love.

And then I think James needed to want to change on his own. I can't live his life for him, but it doesn't mean I give up on him. I, too, have lived in rebellion toward God, and he never gave up on me. The Bible commands me to be Christlike, but how far do I go? I can't save James, and maybe that's the point. God is sovereign, so what happened is the complete will of God.

I still believe that God is the God of this city. I still have a heart to help the poor. The other day a woman with only a couple of teeth in her head walked up to me and asked for money. I noticed her thrift-store slacks and blouse that couldn't pass at any restaurant without getting the weird "you're homeless" stare. Her request didn't provoke the emotional response she desired. I knew she was on drugs. Knowing how meth rots out a person's teeth like termites in an old house, I didn't hesitate to assume the worst.

"You need a bus pass, don't you?" I asked, responding to the usual request of a person doped up and trying to con an unsuspecting citizen.

She looked at me surprised, like, how did I know her story? She thought for a moment and explained that she had a daughter she needed to go and see. She was lying, but I didn't press it. I now had Sherlock Holmesian special powers of observation. I had trained myself to listen to what the poor say and predict how they would manipulate their way into my wallet. Most homeless folks would follow up a bus-pass request with tales of wealth and success about that relative. My inner monologue always asks the question, *Why don't they buy your bus pass?*

I ended up giving her all the change in my pocket—a penny and a quarter. For her, this was good news. She didn't look at the change with disdain but rather as another step closer to her next hit of meth. The hard-core drugs users like her are the same ones you see every day on the exit ramp of the highway or at the busy intersection with signs explaining their plight. They never go away, because they live for the next hit. The cycle goes like this: get high, pass out, wake up, need another hit, find a sign and a busy stoplight, and ask the sympathetic do-gooders to supply the next round. There are some who aren't like that, but odds are that's the deal for the guy with the cardboard sign you see every day and think, *Why don't you get a job?*

Don't hear me say that it's easy to go from being homeless and on drugs to working at UPS, throwing boxes in the back of a truck, and getting health benefits. I know it's not. Dancing through the bureaucracy of the system is difficult. For example, if someone commits a crime and gets a felony at age nineteen, he will serve his five years in prison with time off for good behavior. When he gets out, he's met with the fact that no corporate employer in his right mind would want to hire him. I mean, would you place a felon's resumé on the top of the stack?

However, even in the worst economy, there are jobs. James went through three jobs that I know of. I continue to watch a stream of illegal immigrants gather in parking lots downtown, pursuing work as day laborers, but James never took one of those jobs. It was beneath him.

The main issue still remains: How do you know if someone who has fallen from society has really sought to reform himself? How do you know if he ever really changed or can change? How do you know he won't use you for his own selfish interest to find pleasure in some sort of self-destructive behavior?

I guess that's why I'm so frustrated with the welfare system. It creates a pattern of dependence with no accountability. If you perpetuate this kind of habit, you eventually run out of other people's money and patience. Finally, you can't shut it off without those who are fed by it screaming—loudly. But remember these people are *still* people, made in the image of God.

Those who live off welfare will find another place to get a free lunch, and I believe that should be the church. The church should be abused and taken advantage of by the poor, because perhaps there they might find something greater than government.

In Proverbs 31, King Lemuel's mom was giving her son wisdom. She told him not to chase after women, not to drink in excess, and not to forget the poor. Then she gave him specific instruction about the poor. I did a double take when I first read this.

"Give beer to those who are perishing, wine to those who are in anguish; let them drink and forget their poverty and remember their misery no more."[1]

So the Word of God tells me to give beer to the poor? That seems wrong, doesn't it? Especially if I know for a fact they are just going to do meth, cause their teeth to fall out, and die prematurely. Is that really what God meant?

I don't think we're supposed to host raves or hand out free alcohol and drugs for the homeless to feed their addictions, but I do think we need to give them the grace we've received.

A homeless person's pain is real. It's not contrived. They need help and beer—or some other drug, which is the temporary solution. However, King Lemmie's mom doesn't stop there.

"Speak up for those who cannot speak for themselves, for the rights of all who are destitute. Speak up and judge fairly; defend the rights of the poor and needy."[2]

There is something more here. She wanted her son to take on the burden of the poor and outcast. She wanted him to be responsible for them. Because most likely the reason for drinking is a sense of helplessness when the system is broken and justice is not meted out.

In my church history class at school, Dr. Bingham taught us about excusative versus transformative grace. Essentially, excusative grace is giving to the poor and excusing their self-destructive behavior. Because their lives are about as horrid as one can imagine, and since they are in anguish, you provide a quick fix for the problem by giving them money. They say it's for a bus pass, which really means it's for a drink or a drug, and as a result, they temporarily forget their pain. I like excusative grace because it is convenient, quick, and easy, and my money does the work as opposed to me.

Dr. Bingham said that he is grateful Jesus didn't use that kind of grace. Jesus was into transformative grace. This means Jesus forgives and then actively bears the burden of our sin and all that is involved in the process of transformation. Jesus went to the cross and bore the burden for sin, but he didn't stop there. He is in heaven right now and has been there since he rose from the dead, praying for us and interceding with the Father on our behalf.

In the same way, if we are going to be Jesus to our culture, it's going to cost us. We must die to ourselves and give our lives away in order to see that transformation in others. We must be our brothers' keepers and take a risk that may not be safe or easy.

On the flip side, there will always be those who refuse help. A buddy of mine told me about a homeless couple who slept outside his church in a small gutter. Someone in the church thought it would be great to have the couple sleep inside the church. The homeless couple were grateful for the roof, but as soon as any rules were applied, they decided the gutter was more appealing.

I don't even know where to start with that. I'm searching the Scriptures for answers on this and am finding that wrestling with the text is more important than finding the answer. I don't think we are supposed to line up Scriptures against each other in a small ring and watch them battle it out like a prizefight. Pitting 2 Thessalonians 3:10[3] against Matthew 5:42[4] is not the point. They are both God-breathed Scriptures, never meant to battle one another. They reveal the complete will of God.

Taking care of the poor is not a Republican/Democrat thing. It's something for those who have the Spirit of God. The poor will not be transformed with more money. That only gives them a fish. I challenge the church to arise from isolationist suburbia and start the life-on-life discipleship that is very messy and guaranteed to cost. God has called the church to be responsible for taking care of the poor, needy, and destitute, regardless of whether or not they deserve it. Perhaps a soul will be saved when they see God's hand working through those who care for them. At the very least, Jesus will be pleased with his obedient bride.

We have one core purpose on this earth: to make famous and great the name of our God. Part of that is sharing the hope we have with a lost world that is in desperate need of salvation. We do this through serving them without regard for reciprocity. That is our call from Christ.

A PROCLAMATION FROM THE BOOK OF ISAIAH

"Shout it aloud, do not hold back.
Raise your voice like a trumpet.

Declare to my people their rebellion
and to the house of Jacob their sins.

For day after day they seek me out;
they seem eager to know my ways,

as if they were a nation that does what is right
and has not forsaken the commands of its God.

They ask me for just decisions
and seem eager for God to come near them.

'Why have we fasted,' they say,
'and you have not seen it?

Why have we humbled ourselves,
and you have not noticed?'

"Yet on the day of your fasting, you do as you please
and exploit all your workers.

Your fasting ends in quarreling and strife,
and in striking each other with wicked fists.

You cannot fast as you do today
and expect your voice to be heard on high.

Is this the kind of fast I have chosen,
only a day for a man to humble himself?

Is it only for bowing one's head like a reed
and for lying on sackcloth and ashes?

STUMBLING SOULS

Is that what you call a fast,
a day acceptable to the Lord?

"Is not this the kind of fasting I have chosen:

to loose the chains of injustice
and untie the cords of the yoke,

to set the oppressed free
and break every yoke?

Is it not to share your food with the hungry
and to provide the poor wanderer with shelter—

when you see the naked, to clothe him,
and not to turn away from your own flesh and blood?

Then your light will break forth like the dawn,
and your healing will quickly appear;

then your righteousness will go before you,
and the glory of the Lord will be your rear guard.

Then you will call, and the Lord will answer;
you will cry for help, and he will say: Here am I.

"If you do away with the yoke of oppression,
with the pointing finger and malicious talk,

and if you spend yourselves in behalf of the hungry
and satisfy the needs of the oppressed,

then your light will rise in the darkness,
and your night will become like the noonday."

An extraordinary event manifesting divine intervention in human affairs.

—*Webster's* definition of a miracle

POSTSCRIPT: RESURRECTION

TWO YEARS LATER

I sent this book to the publisher May 30. I had sent James a couple of e-mails asking him if he was okay, but I never heard back. I was hoping to see if he was still living. If so, I hoped to take him to lunch and pray with him. However, I never received a reply, until now.

From: James Rudolph, Jr.
Sent: Thursday, June 25, 2009 9:44 AM
To: Chris Plekenpol

Subject: Re: how have you been?

> Well,
>
> I'm checking my e-mail and who do I come across but you!!! I've been out of the loop because I'm in a discipleship program in Denton called, "Denton Freedom House"!!!!!! Check it out on the web!!!! www.dentonfreedomhouse.org. This place is awesome!!! I really would like to get in touch with you and touch bases with you. There is some stuff that I need to tell you that needs to be said face to face!!! My graduation ceremony from the first phase here is Saturday the 27th and I would like for you to be here!!!
>
> So give me a call today or sometime before tomorrow and let me know if you can come and it will include a free dinner!!! Can't go wrong with free food!!!!!! God has done some major stuff in my life and I need to share it with you!!!! We will also be going to Six Flags on Monday the 29th so hopefully you can join us then also!!! Call me today at ***-***-**** and ask for James Rudolph, Jr. I can come to the phone when you call!!! Call as soon as you get this!!! I'd love to hear from you!!!!!
>
> Love and God Bless!!!
>
> James Rudolph, Jr.

I almost dropped my laptop. I grabbed my cell phone and furiously dialed the number. My hands shook as I listened to the ring across the line.

"Denton Freedom House, this is James."

"James, this is Chris Plekenpol. How are you, man?"

"Oh my God! Chris, this is incredible. I am so glad you called. I graduate on Saturday from phase one of the Denton Freedom House. Can you come?"

"I'll be there."

"I have so much to tell you—I can't talk to you about it now because I have to go, but I will see you there."

"All right, man, see you then."

In an instant everything not only became worth it; it became necessary. God had worked a miracle, and through his providence, I would be there to see the fruit of my labor.

Saturday came, and I made my way north to Denton. After driving over an hour, I arrived at the Freedom House. James called me just as I pulled into the gravel driveway.

"Hey, you still coming?" he asked.

"I'm here, man. Where do I park?" I responded.

I scanned the pasture and the buildings in the middle of nowhere, and then I saw him. James pointed to an open gravel space. I parked the vehicle, got out, and tried to maintain my cool as I approached the man whom I hadn't seen in almost two years.

"Good to see you, man. This is a miracle," I said.

"Yes, it is. God has done something in my life."

I hugged James hard and didn't let emotion overwhelm me. James turned quickly, and I followed him into the Freedom House. He sat me down at a table with a resident named Brian, who looked about twenty-three, and a couple of volunteers.

"I have to do some work, but we will catch up later," he said.

"Do your thing, man."

James quickly busied himself with filling glasses and delivering food to others with a smile on his face. I tried to find the droop, but it was gone.

I learned from Brian that the Freedom House has a rigorous two-phase program to help free men from addiction. The first phase lasts a total of six months. A daily routine involving two hours of manual labor around the Freedom House accompanies intense Bible study. The second phase is re-entry into life outside the program.

To graduate, Brian told me he had to be in the home for a minimum of 180 days, work 180 hours, memorize the mission statement, discipleship model, and complete all of the core curriculum including the Scripture-reading plan, Scripture memory plan, book reports, lessons, and prayer journal.

He also had to fulfill any disciplinary requirements, which he didn't get in to.

After dinner, James took me outside to show me the place. I went back to his room and found the book by Jack Deere, *Surprised by the Voice of God*. We had a quick laugh. He now had his own room, but he used to live with four other guys in the bunkroom.

We went outside, and he showed me the meditation garden that he and the other residents had worked on for the past six months. He showed me the double-wide trailer that had just been donated for Jeremy, the director of the Denton Freedom House, and his family to live in.

The sun had started to set, giving the auburn glow above the tree line. The cicadas chirped, and we both took it in.

"This is a miracle, James."

"Yeah." James paused and looked me in the eye. "I never had the chance to apologize, and I wanted to tell you I'm sorry for everything. I also wanted to thank you for everything."

"No problem, man. I'm just glad to have a bit part in your amazing story. What was the thing that finally convinced you to come here?" I asked.

"They told me I could do all my laundry. Not just a load, but all of it," James said.

I waited to see if he was joking, but he just stared at the sunset. I laughed to myself. *Laundry.*

We went back inside, and James helped finish transforming the dining room into a sanctuary. The white, plastic folding chairs we had just sat on to eat had now become the pews we would rest on as we watched James and two other men graduate from the Freedom House. The small room was the size of a closet in any megachurch today. It was standing room only at the much-anticipated ceremony. Jeremy asked James to set up three chairs facing the gathering. James promptly arose and did as he was told.

Jeremy asked the three men graduating to sit in front of the crowd of around fifty. He introduced himself and thanked all the visitors for being there. He asked one of the men to pray over the evening, and a large black man rose from the back of the room and called upon the Lord with a loud voice.

Jeremy then asked the men to each stand up and give their five-minute testimony of how they arrived at the Freedom House and how Christ changed them. The first two went with similar stories. They were older black men who had run the streets for years, chasing the life of pleasure found in women and drugs. Both had grown up without fathers, and both had come to the end of themselves before they were ready for a change.

Dana, the first man to be recognized, said something that stuck with me: "I have never seen a man like Jeremy. I just like to watch the way he treats his wife and how he loves those kids."

Jeremy then asked James to speak. James showed a video that I'd made over two years ago at Dallas Seminary, which chronicled his life and struggle being homeless, HIV positive, and gay. I had originally made the video thinking that my SPF7 group might be the catalyst to his freedom. After the video, James stood up.

"Well, this all started with that man right there and when he kicked me out." James pointed at me. "We didn't end on good terms, and I was angry and depressed. I fell into a deep depression, and I thought about just jumping off the top of a building when Anthony, right there," James pointed to a young man behind me, "handed me a sandwich and said, 'God still has a plan for you.'"

James then described how a series of different men stepped into his life for a season until he was convinced to come to the Denton Freedom House.

"There were two times I almost left the Freedom House," James said. "I had my bags packed up, and I was heading for the door, and then something just turned me back. This hasn't been easy, but I now feel like I can fulfill my call to ministry."

I couldn't stop smiling.

Jeremy then asked the gathering if anyone had anything to say to the three men.

A man behind me stood up and said, "James, I remember when I first met you. I didn't like you. I didn't like your attitude. But you have become one of the most humble servants I've ever met."

Anthony stood up behind me and cleared his throat. "James, the night I handed you that sandwich, I felt like God was calling me to you. To see you in that depression then and to the smile on your face now can only be described as a God thing."

Person after person stood up and gave a testimony about the James before and the James after. My eyes started to water as I realized God used me in such a small way to make a big change in this man's life. I got to play in the supporting cast in Jesus' story of redemption in one man's life.

James told us that he decided to stay on at the Freedom House as an intern and would give his life to the ministry.

He sat down, and Jeremy asked the mentors of the Denton Freedom House to come and pray over the three graduates. We prayed for their continued growth and strength to stave off temptation. Afterward a small band got up and led worship. I left around ten o'clock; I had a long drive home and was preaching in Fort Worth the following day. I told James I would meet him at Six Flags on Monday.

Monday came, and I met James and four other men at the amusement park. Memories of the last time we both were at Six Flags with Christina and Amanda two years ago resurfaced. Now here we were, riding the rides and screaming our lungs out, homelessness a far distant memory.

I assumed that the other guys who were there all worked in conjunction with the Freedom House. I was wrong. They didn't even know each other, except through James. Anthony had ministered to James right after he left me. Nick and his parents had been a part of a ministry that fed the homeless and allowed James to be a part of their work on their streets. Troy was an engineer who attended Richard Ellis's church, Reunion Church, and he had gotten to know James through that and had been able to meet with and encourage James. And there was Ryan, who had gotten James job after job only to watch him lose whatever job he got time and time again. Ryan looked at me while waiting to go on the Titan.

"I really wondered if I was just wasting my time. I really did. He didn't care enough to keep the job. It was frustrating. I lost track of James for over six months when I went on a mission trip to South America and came back and couldn't find him. I just got an e-mail a couple of days ago telling me he was at the Freedom House."

"Wait, you mean, you don't know these people?" I asked.

"No, we all just met. That's why this is so awesome."

My heart leaped into my throat. "Wow," I managed.

Many are the plans in a man's heart, but it is the Lord's
purpose that prevails.
What a man desires is unfailing love.

—from the Book of Proverbs

TODAY

James and I preached at a homeless shelter recently, and it was incredible to see these men respond to James and his story. There is something powerful when someone can look at those who are on the other side of recovery and see hope in the eyes of one who made it. If you had asked me the day I originally sent this manuscript to my publisher the odds of James being the man who discipled guys needing rehab and spoke with me to the hurting, I would have said: one in a million. I am amazed James is even alive today. However, he's more than physically living; he's a man spiritually alive with God working through him and for him for the kingdom. I don't want to paint a picture perfect image of James. He is still James and I am still me. We argue. We disagree. We snap at each other. I have picked him up from the library downtown after he felt he was mistreated by the Freedom House. But no one quit on James. Ryan, Troy, John, and I, the same men who walked him through his time of homelessness before the Freedom House, are still here to walk him through his time at the Freedom House. I don't think we ever get to put the ribbon on our lives and say we've arrived.

The question "Is love enough?" subtitles this book. I've found that our human love isn't perfect. Selfishness and pride leave much to be desired, and, therefore, our love is never enough.

David writes in the Psalms over and over again about this concept of unfailing love. He wants a love that will love him despite himself—despite knowing David fully.

I don't have the ability to love unconditionally outside of Christ. That is why the only love that will ever be enough is the love of God. He gave his only Son to die on a cross for the sins of the world, and then he gets involved in the mess of ministry, of our working out our salvation with fear and trembling, by using flawed people to piece together another person's redemption so that only he gets the glory. That allows me to trust him that he really does have the whole world in his hands. I don't know if you noticed it, but there were a couple of times when I enjoyed the pats on the backs and the acknowledgment that *I* was doing something for God. I realized through this God doesn't need me, but if we approach him with a humble heart and prayer, he will use us. Pride is tricky, and I always have to be on guard against my flesh.

I said earlier in the epilogue that this was still worth it even if James hadn't been able to see the light. God used my life in a way that honored Christ. I also learned that all I can do is serve him by opening up my doors for those who are needy and close them for those who need to experience the "far country" and feel the discipline and grace of God for themselves. I can plant, you can water, but God is the one who makes it grow.

I am learning this with the guys I have taken to James at the Freedom House. I took one kid into my home for a couple of months, trying to give him a new start. I met this twenty-three-year-old while preaching in Panama City Beach, Florida. He was living the party dream when conviction swept over his heart, and he wanted a new start. He asked if he could live with me.

I thought it over for about a minute; he couldn't be any worse than James, so I said yes. After four months, he couldn't get over the cocaine and crack, so I brought him directly to the Denton Freedom House to get help. He didn't make it. After a month, he quit and went to live with his father. We are still friends, and I visit him every now and then. He is doing better now, and although I wish he stuck it out like James and finished, I know God isn't through with him. I can't get down just because God didn't bring an increase that I can see.

The other kid I brought to James was the result of parents hearing about my mentoring teens and young adults. They begged me to talk to their son. After a couple of meetings I handed him off to James. He is sticking it out at the Freedom House—so far. Only God's love is enough. For those who receive it, it is more than enough; for those who don't, it is merely a nice philosophy that worked for someone else.

I don't know if you watched the progression of my growth as you read this book. I went from a Christian ideologue to a person who has an understanding of life on the streets and an understanding of how Christ makes believers righteous on the basis of grace, by means of faith. Did you see me grow? I can't help but notice the difference. I have more compassion. I have a deeper love for the lost. I have a better grasp at how rotten I can be in my own sufficiency. There wasn't just one stumbling soul in this book; my sins were pretty apparent, and God is still working on my selfishness and pride. I know that with God all things are possible.

So I watch for God's hand to reveal his heart in redeeming people. I don't have to look hard to see what God will do to woo his people back to himself. I want to be involved in that. I want my life to be second to the movement of putting the agenda of our heavenly Father first in everything that we do.

ENDNOTES

CHAPTER 2
1. Luke 14:12–14

CHAPTER 5
1. Hebrews 10:24

CHAPTER 6
1. James 2:15–17

CHAPTER 11
1. Ephesians 1:11 NET

CHAPTER 12
1. "For he himself is our peace, who has made the two one and has destroyed the barrier, the dividing wall of hostility, by abolishing in his flesh the law with its commandments and regulations. His purpose was to create in himself one new man out of the two, thus making peace."

CHAPTER 13
1. James 2:13–17 NASB

STUMBLING SOULS

CHAPTER 18
1. James 4:17 NASB

CHAPTER 19
1. Matthew 7:1–5 NET

CHAPTER 24
1. Mark 8:34–35

CHAPTER 25
1. Matthew 10:27 NET

CHAPTER 26
1. James 5:16–18

CHAPTER 32
1. 1 Corinthians 1:20–21

CHAPTER 36
1. Charles E. Hummel popularized a helpful phrase in the title of his book *Tyranny of the Urgent* (Downers Grove, IL: InterVarsity Press, 1967, 1994).

CHAPTER 39
1. Romans 7:15
2. C. S. Lewis, *The Weight of Glory*, (New York: HarperCollins, 2001), 26.

EPILOGUE
1. Proverbs 31:6–7
2. Proverbs 31:8–9
3. "For even when we were with you, we gave you this rule: 'If a man will not work, he shall not eat.'"
4. "Give to the one who asks you, and do not turn away from the one who wants to borrow from you."

I AM SECOND®

I am Second® is a movement meant to inspire people of all kinds to live for God and for others. Actors. Athletes. Musicians. Business leaders. Drug addicts. Your next-door neighbor. People like you. The authentic stories on iamsecond.com provide insight into dealing with typical struggles of everyday living. These are stories that give hope to the lonely and the hurting, help from destructive lifestyles, and inspiration to the unfulfilled. You'll discover people who've tried to go it alone and have failed. Find the hope, peace, and fulfillment they found. Be Second. Use I am Second tools to help love your communities to Christ.

I am Second is designed to help people discover their purpose in life. Have you discovered yours? **Visit iamsecond.com.**

How can you get involved?

I am Second® is designed to spark spiritual conversations to discover how to live Second by making Jesus First. There are many ways to get started:

Pray Download or order our prayer guide that teaches people how to connect deeper with God and see the world as He does.

Care Start I am Second service groups and be the hands and feet of Jesus in your community. Go through the GoLocal small group discussion guides and use the Street Tools (t-shirts, bumper stickers, business cards, wrist-bands) to draw attention to your GoLocal project. Simply go to **iamsecond.com/getinvolved** and click **Buy Stuff**.

Share Start an I am Second group to reach your friends, neighbors, and co-workers. Small group discussion guides available via download or order on our website. Take it a step further and go international on an I am Second Expedition, powered by e3 Partners.

Visit iamsecond.com.

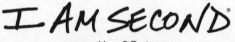

powered by e3 Partners

info@iamsecond.com